DEAD MEN TALKING

DEAD MEN TALKING

Afterlife Communication From World War I

by

MICHAEL TYMN

www.whitecrowbooks.com

Published and printed in the United States of America and the United Kingdom
by White Crow Books; an imprint of White Crow Productions Ltd.

For information, contact White Crow Books
at 3 Merrow Grange, Guildford, GU1 2QW United Kingdom,
or e-mail to info@whitecrowbooks.com.

Cover Designed by Butterflyeffect
Interior design by Velin@Perseus-Design.com

Paperback ISBN 978-1-910121-13-9
eBook   ISBN 978-1-910121-14-6

Non Fiction / Body, Mind & Spirit / Death & Dying

www.whitecrowbooks.com

The shock of the war was meant to rouse us to mental and moral earnestness, to give us the courage to tear away venerable shams, and to force the human race to realize and use the vast new revelation which has been so clearly stated and so abundantly proved, for all who will examine the statements and proofs with an open mind.

— Sir Arthur Conan Doyle

Few families have not been struck down by some calamity during the years of war. I want to point out that death is not so serious a matter – it is transition, a natural process of emancipation of the soul from the body – dissolution but not extinction. When people think of the body living in the grave, they should not think of the person as associated with that body. The body is only a transitory thing of 70 or 80 years, but that which has grown within that body will perish. We must think of the transitoriness of the body and the permanence of the soul. It is necessary to realize that character is a possession which lasts throughout eternity. That character we form here, we take with us, we cannot get away from it. Suicide does not help at all. We only take ourselves with us into the next life, nothing else.

Death by violence is a calamity, but do not mourn unduly for those that are gone, for, as Macaulay says, "They were in some sort happy in the opportunity of their death." This kind of death has in it an element of sacrifice, of redemption, which we may hope will be accounted to them. Let us realize the magnitude and complexity of the universe. Perhaps we may yet find that it is our bodily disability which prevents us seeing the vast amount of intelligence and help working with us. Let us try to think of those who are gone as not really gone, but unseen by us, in a glorious scheme of help and pity. We must change to something higher. The angels keep their ancient order and we do not know what we shall become, but there are all grades of being up from man to Deity. This vision is not purely imaginary. The great men of the race are not deceived, and they say even more than we do.

— Sir Oliver Lodge

Other books by the author:
The Articulate Dead
Running on Third Wind
The Afterlife Revealed
The Afterlife Explorers Vol. 1
Transcending the Titanic
Resurrecting Leonora Piper

CONTENTS

PREFACE

A DOOR AJAR

As Rolf Little tells his mother in Chapter Five of this book, the "door" between the material world and the spirit world was opened 2,000 years ago, but people didn't really follow the teachings that came through that door and therefore it closed, opening only intermittently in the centuries that followed. However, the anguish and despair that accompanied the physical deaths of more than 16-million people in the "Great War" of 1914-1918 created a "thought force" that propped it open and put at least a temporary wedge in it.

During that time, many warriors who had "Gone West," as death on the battlefield was called, communicated with loved ones left behind through mediums, telling them they were still "alive," though not in the flesh, and that the loved ones should not grieve. This book is an anthology of five books (seven, including two sequels), all abridged, coming out of World War I, detailing communication with discarnate soldiers. They are:

> *Raymond or Life and Death* and *Raymond Revised*
> *Thy Son Liveth: Messages from a Soldier to his Mother*
> *Claude's Book I* and *Claude's Book II*
> *Private Dowding*
> *Rolf's Life in the Spirit World*

Raymond, Bob, Claude, Thomas, and Rolf all reported that they had not found themselves in some humdrum heaven or in an abyss of nothingness but rather in a world that seemed very much like the material world they had just left. There was initially some confusion as they awakened to their new reality, and there was a period of adjustment in which they were assisted by guides, sometimes relatives who had transitioned before them. All were surprised at the nature of the afterlife condition, saying it was nothing like they had expected. Probably the primary message from all was that the afterlife is made up of many realms, planes, or spheres, and that, upon physical death, we transition to the realm we have prepared ourselves for during the earth life. In effect, our actions and deeds in this life result in what has been called a "moral specific gravity," which determines where we begin the next life – the *real* life, the one this life was designed to prepare us for.

Indications are that most people – those not particularly materialistic and selfish, yet not especially advanced in spiritual ways – begin on what is referred to as the third sphere, sometimes called Summerland, where conditions are not too unlike those of the earth realm, though of a higher vibration and therefore less materialistic and mechanistic. The more materialistic and selfish people find themselves "earthbound" in the first sphere, often not even realizing they are "dead," or in something of a stupor in the second sphere, depending on the moral specific gravity. It was often stressed that those who find themselves in those lowly states – what might be called a "fire of the mind," i.e., the hell of religion – are not there for eternity as taught by many religions. They are able to advance to higher realms following a plan of spiritual evolution.

The more advanced soul might awaken on the fourth sphere, or a higher one. The seventh sphere is said to be the highest, although the numbering system is apparently somewhat arbitrary and symbolic for the benefit of human understanding. Conditions from the fourth sphere on up are said to be increasingly beyond human comprehension, but many spirit messengers have communicated that as we advance toward Oneness with the Creator that we retain our individuality.

Most books on life after death are focused either on the evidence supporting a belief in the survival of consciousness or on the nature of the afterlife. My books, *The Articulate Dead*, *The Afterlife Explorers*, and *Resurrecting Leonora Piper*, are more of the first type, while my book *The Afterlife Revealed*, is of the second type. Another book, *Transcending the Titanic*, is more about facing death. This book is more of the second type, although the first chapter, that about Raymond Lodge, offers some intriguing evidence strongly suggesting life after death, enough evidence to convince Raymond's father, Sir Oliver Lodge, a world renowned scientist of a century ago, that his son was communicating with him through a credible medium. As further discussed in the introductory paragraphs of Chapter One, debunkers then and now were/are convinced that Sir Oliver was a victim of fraud and his own wishful thinking resulting from grief, but anyone taking the time to examine his many writings will discover that he began to believe in a future life some 16 years before Raymond's death on the battlefield.

"The verification of the fact of telepathy, indicating obscurely a kind of dislocation between mind and body, was undoubtedly impressive, so that it began to seem probable, especially under [Frederic] Myers's tuition, that the two – mind and body – were not inseparably connected, as I had been led by my previous studies under Clifford, Tyndall, and Huxley to believe they were," Lodge explained his conversion. "I began to feel that there was a possibility of the survival of personality.

"Then came the revelation, through the mediumship of Mrs. Piper, in the winter of 1889, not only that the personality of certain people could survive, but that they could communicate under certain conditions with us. The proof that they retained their individuality, their memory, and their affection, forced itself upon me, as it had done upon many others. So my eyes began to open to the fact that there really was a spiritual world, as well as a material world, which hitherto had seemed all sufficient, that the things which appealed to the senses were by no means the whole of existence."

To his many colleagues in the scientific world – the scientific fundamentalists who were unable to distinguish between the superstitions and follies of organized religion and the information coming to Lodge through mediums, Lodge countered the criticism by saying, "Science is incompetent to make comprehensive denials about anything. It should not deal in the negative. Denial is no more fallible than assertion. There are cheap and easy kinds of skepticism, just as there are cheap and easy kinds of dogmatism."

Even though Rolf Little said that Jesus "opened the door," he must have meant "reopened" it, as mediumship in its various forms has been taking place for at least as long as recorded history, probably since the first humans inhabited the earth. The Bible is filled with stories of spirit communication, although modern translations usually refer to spirits as angels, messengers, or the Holy Ghost and to the mediums as prophets or seers. Moses's receiving of the Ten Commandments (Ex. 20:1-17) appears to be an example of the direct-writing form of mediumship, while Samuel is called from the dead through the medium of Endor (Sam. 28: 3-21). Other examples are Balaam (Num. 22:23-36) and Hagar (Gen. 16:7-15), who encountered "angels" with important messages.

Unfortunately, organized religion has given negative interpretations to mediumship, referring to the medium of Endor as a "witch" and conveniently citing passages in the Old Testament seemingly forbidding the consulting of mediums while ignoring or giving different interpretations to passages in the New Testament that appear to sanction mediumship. For example, one is advised to "test" the mediums, whether they are of God (1 John 4:1) and to "discern" the messages (Cor. 12:10). How is one to test and discern if he does not listen to them in the first place? And, if some are from God, why are they to be avoided?

Perhaps in anticipation of the Civil War in the United States, the door began to creak open in 1848, triggered by an event that came to be known as the "Rochester knockings," communication coming by means of knocks and raps – so many knocks or raps for each letter of the alphabet, or the sitters would recite the alphabet and the spirit communicator would knock or rap at the desired letter, slowly spelling out a message.

In spite of limited mass communication in those days, the story of the Rochester knockings spread rapidly and turned into an epidemic of spirit communication. Mediums began developing in all parts of the United States as well as in Europe. The phenomena progressed from rappings and tappings to table tilting and turning and table levitations. The table phenomena usually involved sitters placing their hands on the table and the table lifting off the floor, although there were many observations of the table tilting, turning, or lifting independently of any hands. The spirit communicators would then respond to the questions by tilts of the table instead of knocks or raps. The "madness," as some referred to it, came to be called "Spiritualism."

If the spirits who communicated in the years immediately following the Rochester knockings are to be believed, there was a plan behind it all – a plan that resulted from a growing loss of faith and spiritual values in an increasingly materialistic world. Certain advanced spirits were chosen, early investigators were informed, to communicate with humans and give them a better idea of man's purpose and destiny. According to spirit messages, the rapping method of communication was discovered by Benjamin Franklin and Emanuel Swedenborg working together in the spirit world. Rappings had been noticed well before the

Rochester knockings, but apparently no one thought to consider them as a means of spirit communication. As William Stainton Moses, an Anglican priest who became a renowned medium, was informed, in earlier times spirits communicated with men in ways less material, but as men grew more corporeal it became necessary for a material system of telegraphy to be invented. It also became increasingly clear that the communicating spirits have as many obstacles to overcome in communicating with us as we have in communicating with them.

The spiritualism epidemic gave rise to much fraud. Even the Fox sisters, the mediums for the original Rochester knockings, were apparently under pressure to produce results on every occasion after coming under the management of showman P. T. Barnum, and are said to have used tricks when the spirits were silent, and later in life, when destitute, one of them accepted money from a newspaper to admit to fraud. However, it was clear to serious investigators that much of the phenomena could not have been faked.

Among the dedicated and distinguished pioneering psychical researchers were:

- John Edmonds, Chief Justice of the New York State Supreme Court
- Robert Hare, professor of chemistry at the University of Pennsylvania and renowned inventor
- Allan Kardec, French educator and author
- Alfred Russel Wallace, biologist and co-originator with Charles Darwin of the natural selection theory of evolution
- William Crookes, chemist who discovered the element thallium and was a pioneer in x-ray technology, later knighted for his contributions to science
- William Barrett, professor of physics at the Royal College in Dublin and inventor, later knighted for his contributions to science.

Each of these men began as a skeptic but became a believer in the reality of mediumship and in spirit communication. Barrett was instrumental in the formation of the Society for Psychical Research, an organization formed to investigate psychic phenomena, in 1882. Five years later, he would encourage the formation of the American branch of the SPR (ASPR). Among the scholars and scientists who joined the

SPR and ASPR and became dedicated researchers in those early years were:

- William James, professor of philosophy, psychology, and medicine at Harvard University, one of the pioneers of modern psychology
- Oliver Lodge, professor of physics and pioneer in electricity and radio, later knighted for his contributions to science
- Charles Richet, professor of physiology and winner of the 1913 Nobel Prize in medicine and physiology
- Camille Flammarion, pioneer in astronomy and founder of the French Astronomical Society
- Cesare Lombroso, Italian psychiatrist and founder of the science of criminology
- James H. Hyslop, professor of logic and ethics at Columbia University and pioneer in abnormal psychology.

While these researchers and others came to believe in the reality of psychic phenomena, including mediumship, the materialistic/mechanistic philosophy was much too strong in its resistance. During the late 1890s and into the 1900s, interest in mediumship began to wane. The "door" remained ajar, but blew wide open again, as Rolf suggested, with the Great War and its millions of casualties. But, following the war, scientific and technical advances brought a return to the more materialistic ways of life and the door again shut, or at least remained only slightly ajar. There are indications that it is slowly creaking open again, but the antagonistic forces – the fundamentalists of both mainstream science and orthodox religion – continue to exert strong pressure against the door.

Nevertheless, some seeds blew through the door during the mediumship that took place during the Great War, enough to sprout and provide nourishment for future generations if they choose to awaken to the reality of it all. It is to the cultivation of those seeds that this book has been inspired and is now dedicated.

Michael Tymn
April 2, 2014

INTRODUCTION

UNDERSTANDING SPIRIT COMMUNICATION

L isa Williams, a popular television medium, had two sisters and a brother in tears as she passed on some very evidential messag-es from their deceased mother on one of her programs. At the end of the reading, Ms. Williams asked them if they had any questions before she lost contact with their mother. One of the young women asked if her mother had given her name. Ms Williams responded that she had not, and made no attempt to explain the problem in getting the mother's name.

One could easily imagine the belly laughs of all the skeptics who might have been watching the program. Here is this supposed medium passing on all this information and she can't get a simple name. "How absolutely ridiculous!" "What a sham!"

Of course, if the skeptics had stopped to think about it, the failure to get a name actually lends credibility to Ms. Williams. After all, if the claim is that she researched in advance all the evidential informa-tion she passed on to the sitters, why wouldn't she have known the name of their mother? Such reasoning, however, is usually beyond the grasp of the skeptics.

Gladys Osborne Leonard (1882 – 1968), the primary medium the reader will meet in this book (Chapters One, Three, and Five) was not the same kind of medium as Lisa Williams. While Ms. Williams is con-sidered a clairvoyant, Mrs. Leonard was primarily a trance-speaking medium. However, their difficulties with getting names and certain words seem to have been similar.

Mrs. Leonard was studied extensively by scientists and scholars representing the Society for Psychical Research (SPR) and is now considered one of the greatest mediums in the annals of psychical research. She was referred to as "England's white crow" and the "British Mrs. Piper," both references being to Leonora Piper, an American trance medium who preceded Mrs. Leonard by nearly three decades and was referred to by Professor William James of Harvard as his "white crow" – the one who proved that all crows are not black.

Some of the very best evidence for the survival of consciousness after death came through Mrs. Leonard's mediumship. Yet, while preparing this book, I came upon something that made me both curious and a little suspicious.

In reading the transcripts of communication from Claude Kelway-Bamber, a British airman who was killed during World War I, to his mother through Mrs. Leonard's mediumship (Chapter Three), I was puzzled by the fact that Claude occasionally addressed his mother as "darling." While I had recognized the use of this term of endearment between spouses and also directed from parent to child, I had never before heard a son call his mother by such an affectionate term.

What made me especially suspicious was another transcript in which Rolf Little, the subject of Chapter Five, while also communicating through Mrs. Leonard, called his mother "darling." That might be enough for a debunker to cry "fraud" and for a parapsychologist to say it was all coming from Mrs. Leonard's subconscious, not from spirits of the dead.

I wondered if such a term of endearment might be common in England or have been more common in the early 1900s, when the communication took place. I discussed it with Dr. Howard Jones, a British educator and scientist, who said he had never heard it applied to a parent by a child.

After pondering on it for awhile, the explanation dawned on me. As psychical researchers came to understand, the spirit communicator impresses an "idea" on the mind of the medium, while the medium's subconscious mind puts words to the idea. Thus, both Claude and Rolf may have communicated special affection toward their mothers, that when filtered through Mrs. Leonard's brain, came out "darling." With another medium, it might have come out "mother dear."

Professor James Hyslop, a pioneering psychical researcher, explained it this way: "We do not know in detail all that goes on, but we can conceive that a mental picture in the mind of a communicator is transmitted, perhaps telepathically, to the psychic (medium) or to the control. Even though we do not know how this occurs, we can understand why the message takes the form that it does in the mind of the psychic and why the whole process assumes the form of a description of visual, or a report of auditory images...It is apparent that the pictographic process introduces into the communication various sources of mistake and confusion, and thus explains much that the ordinary man with his view of the messages cannot understand. Mental pictures have to be interpreted, either by the control or by the subconscious of the psychic, probably by both."

The "control" referred to by Hyslop, is the "medium" in the spirit world. As researchers came to understand, very few spirits have the ability to communicate directly through a trance medium. Thus, a medium is needed on their side as well in order to facilitate the communication. Mrs. Leonard's "control," called "Feda" for short, would get the message from Claude, Rolf, or whoever was communicating, and then impress the idea on Mrs. Leonard's brain. In effect, there were four parties – the spirit communicator (Rolf, Claude, etc.) , the spirit control (Feda), the medium (Mrs. Leonard), and the "sitter" (Claude and Rolf's mothers, etc.).

Indications were that Feda got the message telepathically from the spirit communicators on their side of the veil, and that she sometimes misinterpreted what they were saying. Thus, there was distortion even before it was impressed upon Mrs. Leonard's brain. But then the message could be further distorted as it was filtered through her brain. Nevertheless, the gist or essence of the messages usually got through, even if the words came from Mrs. Leonard's vocabulary.

As various researchers pointed out, Feda committed many grammatical gaffes in relaying messages from spirit communicators. Moreover, she would often refer to herself in the third person, e.g., "Feda doesn't understand what Raymond is saying," and she would usually relay messages from the spirit communicators as if they were giving them directly, rather than through her. While Sir Oliver Lodge, a famous British physicist who authored the book abridged in Chapter One, left a few of the grammatical errors in the transcripts, apparently for effect, he and other researchers, as well as the authors of the books abridged in Chapters Three and Five, corrected most errors, probably as they were recorded in shorthand, and otherwise smoothed out the language.

Communicating through the renowned automatic writing medium Geraldine Cummins, Frederic W. H. Myers, one of the founders of the Society for Psychical Research in 1882, who died in 1901, stated: "We communicate an impression through the inner mind of the medium. It receives the impression in a curious way. It has to contribute to the body of the message; we furnish the spirit of it. In other words, we send the thoughts and the words usually in which they must be framed, but the actual letters or spelling of the words are drawn from the medium's memory. Sometimes we only send the thoughts and the medium's unconscious mind clothes them in words."

On another occasion, Myers explained it this way: "The inner mind is very difficult to deal with from this side. We impress it with our message. We never impress the brain of the medium directly. That is out of the question. But the inner mind receives our message and sends it on to the brain. The brain is the mere mechanism. The inner mind is like soft wax, it receives our thoughts, their whole content, but it must produce the words to clothe it."

Myers also offered that when discarnate beings want to communicate through a sensitive, they must enter a dream or subjective state which detaches them from the memory of concrete facts in their past lives. "Further, if we communicate directly through the medium, though we often retain our personality [and] our manner of speech, we are frequently unable to communicate through the medium's hand or voice many exact facts about our past career on earth, sometimes not even our own names."

Well before Myers communicated through Geraldine Cummins, he communicated with Sir Oliver Lodge through the trance mediumship of Rosalie Thompson, Lodge recorded that Myers struggled in his initial attempts to communicate. "Lodge, it is not as easy as I thought in my impatience," Myers explained his difficulty after some delay. "Gurney says I am getting on first rate. But I am short of breath." Gurney, who died in 1888, was a co-founder of the Society for Psychical Research with Myers. The "shortness of breath" apparently was a metaphorical shortness of breath. One spirit likened spirit communication to trying to hold one's breath under water and communicate by hand signals with another underwater swimmer.

Myers was just beginning to better appreciate the obstacles that spirits face in their attempts to communicate. "Tell them I am more stupid than some of those I deal with," he continued as he struggled to remember the last time he had seen Lodge. He mentioned that he could not remember many things, not even his mother's name. He went on to say that he felt like he was looking at a misty picture and that he could hear himself using Thompson's voice but that he didn't feel as if he were actually speaking. "It is funny to hear myself talking when it is not myself talking," he went on. "It is not my whole self talking. When I am awake I know where I am."

Years later, Myers again communicated with Lodge and told him that that he was invisible to Feda and had difficulty getting his name through to her. "But at last success was mine," he communicated. "... I do not know which letter first met with her attention. I merely gave the suggestion of my Christian name and surname in letters, and I understood that the first letter was apprehended separately. "To me it is of little moment what first caught her attention; the image really was the sum of myself as I was then alive. Many figures in that sum were not perceived, were not snared in the [psychic] net, but sufficiency was obtained and then she was able to get the name."

After Dr. Richard Hodgson, another researcher, died in 1905, he began communicating through the mediumship of Leonora Piper, whom he had studied for 18 years. "I find now difficulties such as a blind man would experience in trying to find his hat," the surviving consciousness of Hodgson told Professor William Newbold in a July 23, 1906 sitting. "And I am not wholly conscious of my own utterances because they come out automatically, impressed upon the machine (Piper's body)...I impress my thoughts on the machine which registers them at random, and which are at times doubtless difficult to understand. I understand so much better the *modus operandi* than I did when I was in your world."

In 1917, the Rev Charles Drayton Thomas, a respected psychical researcher and Methodist minister, began studying Mrs. Leonard's mediumship. He quickly made contact with his deceased father, John D. Thomas, and his deceased sister, Etta, receiving much veridical information proving their identities. However, he wondered why they had such difficulty in giving their names and the names of others. The discarnate Thomas explained to his son the difficulties involved in communicating names: "One cannot sometimes get the names right. If I wish to speak about a man named "Meadow," I may try that name and find that "Meadow" is not spoken rightly by Feda. So I then wait and try to insert the idea of a green field, connecting it with the idea of the man described. We always try for a definite thing which will tell you exactly what we mean; but if we are unable to do that, we have to get as near to it as we can. Sometimes we have to depend upon slender links in giving you the clue."

As another example, the discarnate Thomas mentioned that when he tried to get the name "Jerusalem" through Feda, she gave the word "Zion" instead. Etta explained to her brother that it was much easier to send ideas to Feda than it was to send words. She said that she could not get her husband's name, "Whitfield," through Feda. "Is it not strange that I cannot say my husband's name?" she asked. "I can feel it, but cannot say it; that is, I cannot get it spoken. I get it on the surface, so to speak, but cannot get it into the medium's mind."

At a sitting four months later, Etta again attempted to get her husband's name through, but only succeeded in getting the medium to say, "Wh, Whi-, Whit-". Etta further explained to her brother that the more she tried to think on the name, the more difficult it was to get it through the medium's brain, adding that she could not control the medium's power of expression. "One may get a word into her mind and yet be unable to make her express it," she explained. "Because it is in the mind, it does not follow that her brain will take it. Unless the ideas in the mind are tapped on to the actual brain, one cannot express them."

Thomas noticed that Feda could more easily catch a first syllable than a whole name, but sometimes she would catch only the first letter, which he understood was pictured for her by the communicator. When one communicating entity tried to get the word 'Greek' through, Feda struggled with "G-, Gre-, Grek, Greg, Greeg."

Thomas further observed that when Feda had latitude in the selection of words, e.g., "Zion" for "Jerusalem," communication was easier. However, when it came to proper names, this alternative was not always possible. The discarnate Thomas also told his son that when he entered the conditions of a sitting his memory would divide into its former earthly conditions of conscious and subconscious. Thus, the same forgetfulness he might have had when in the flesh with regard to names and other things still existed on his side of the veil.

Soon after his death in 1925, Sir William Barrett, a physicist and also a pioneering psychical researcher, began communicating with his wife, Dr. Florence Barrett, through Mrs. Leonard. Lady Barrett wondered why her deceased husband got the name William through, and not "Will," as she had called him and as he had called himself. Also, he addressed her as "Florence,' although he had called her "Flo" when alive. The formality of it made her question whether it was in fact her deceased husband communicating, even though he provided some very evidential information which she concluded no one else could have known.

On November 5, 1929, Sir William explained: "When I come into the conditions of a sitting I then know that I can only carry with me – contain in me – a small portion of my consciousness. The easiest things to lay hold of are what we may call ideas. [However], a detached word, a proper name, has no link with a train of thought except in the detached sense; that is far more difficult than any other feat of memory or association of ideas. If you go to a medium that is new to us, I can make myself known by giving you through that medium an impression of my character and personality, my work on earth, and so forth. Those can all be suggested by thought, impressions, ideas."

Sir William went on to explain that it is extremely difficult to get his nickname through because it is a detached word. "If I wanted to express an idea of my scientific interests I could do it in twenty different ways. I should probably begin by showing books, then giving impressions of the nature of the book and so on, till I had built up a character impression of myself." But single, detached words, he reiterated, were a real problem.

When Sir Arthur Conan Doyle, the physician who created "Sherlock Holmes," was told by a spirit entity known as "'Pheneas" that there was a fellow on his side who had played cricket with him, Sir Arthur requested his name. "Names are terribly difficult," Pheneas responded. "You see, a name does not represent any sort of idea. It is an indigestible chunk. You can't suggest it to the medium's brain. But I will try." Through the medium, in this case, Lady Doyle, Pheneas then wrote a series of letters ending in CINI. It made no sense to Sir Arthur, and no further attempt was made to get the name. However, he later found out that a cricket player named Paravicini had died two days earlier, although neither he nor the medium knew of the death at the time of the sitting. Whether this was Paravicini attempting to communicate, Sir Arthur could not determine for certain. At a later sitting, Pheneas could not get the name of a man he said had been helping Sir Arthur. "Names are extraordinary," he communicated through the medium. "They are like a bubble that is burst. You cannot get the parts together again, because they are not."

In addition to trance mediumship, Mrs. Leonard was also a "table" medium. Table-tilting was a more accurate method of getting names, Drayton Thomas explained, pointing out that the communicator could dispense with the control and, assuming enough psychic energy, direct the tilting personally – so many tilts for each letter of the alphabet or a tilt for the proper letter when the sitter recited the alphabet. But this method was, of course, very slow and cumbersome.

Clearly, there are obstacles to communication with the Spirit World. "You have to reduce spirit to matter, two entirely different forms of expression," explained Silver Birch, the spirit guide who spoke through British medium Maurice Barbanell, "and in that process of stepping down, many things can go wrong."

When I first read *Claude's Book*, the subject of Chapter Three, some 20 years ago, I was in awe of the messages. They made so much sense and were more comprehensive than anything I had previously read, but I questioned whether Claude, only 20 when he transitioned, could have acquired such wisdom and knowledge in such a short period of time after his death. I concluded that much of it was coming from the subconscious of Mrs. Leonard, the medium. At the same time, it did not seem to me that Mrs. Leonard had the training or education to so philosophize. I considered the possibility that her higher self was an advanced soul or that Claude was actually an advanced soul who died prematurely after accomplishing what was intended for him in those short 20 years, but the possibility that Claude was strictly a low-level intermediary passing on messages from higher intelligences now seems more likely to me. Indications are that these higher intelligences are often "group souls" communicating under a single adopted name, as discussed below.

✻✻✻

It was during December 1910 that Mrs. Leonard and two friends began experimenting with the table-tilting method of communicating with spirits. After numerous failures, they finally received messages from several people, including Mrs. Leonard's mother. These messages were spelled out by the table tilting so many times for each letter of the alphabet. During this first successful sitting, a long name was spelled out, beginning with "F." As they could not pronounce it, they asked if they could abbreviate it by drawing several letters from it. The communicating entity consented and the three women selected "F-E-D-A" as the name for the entity.

Feda told them that she was Mrs. Leonard's great-great grandmother, a Hindu by birth, and that she was raised by a Scottish family. She married William Hamilton, Mrs. Leonard's great-great grandfather, at the age of 13 and died soon thereafter, about 1800, while giving birth to a son. Leonard recalled hearing a story about an Indian ancestress from her mother, but did not remember any details. Feda told Mrs. Leonard that she was going to control her as she had work to do through her because of a great happening (apparently World War I) that would soon take place. Feda further told Mrs. Leonard that she had been with her as a spirit guide since her birth and that she was fulfilling work required of her to make spiritual progress of her own soul.

Initially, Mrs. Leonard refused, telling Feda that the idea of being controlled while in the trance state did not appeal to her. While Feda was disappointed, she continued to come regularly in the table sittings conducted by the three young women. During one table sitting, about 18 months after Feda first introduced herself to them, Mrs. Leonard went into a trance and Feda spoke through her, bringing many messages from friends in the spirit world. As her health was not affected by the trance state, Mrs. Leonard permitted Feda to control her in future sittings, but it took another 18 months before Feda was proficient in taking over Mrs. Leonard's body. Feda then told Mrs. Leonard to become a professional medium and promised her that she would look after her. Mrs. Leonard began by holding circles in Western London, but after the war broke out Feda asked her to give up her public sittings and begin private sittings for those who had lost loved ones in battle.

Drayton Thomas, who had many sittings with Mrs. Leonard, beginning in April 1917, described a typical sitting: Mrs. Leonard would take a seat several feet from him and after two or three minutes of silence she would go into a trance. Suddenly, in a clear and distinct voice, Feda would take over her body and begin using her speech mechanism. There was no similarity between Mrs. Leonard's voice and that of Feda, who spoke like a young girl with a high-pitched voice. Moreover, Feda spoke with an accent and, unlike Mrs. Leonard, had those frequent lapses of grammar.

Occasionally, just after Mrs. Leonard went into the trance state, the sitters would hear whispering of which they could catch fragments, such as, "Yes, Mr. John, Feda will tell him...Yes, all right..." As earlier mentioned, Feda often referred to herself in the third person, e.g., "Feda says she is having trouble understanding Mr. John."

Generally, Feda relayed messages from deceased loved ones, but occasionally she turned over control of Mrs. Leonard to spirits who had the ability to control and communicate directly and in whom she had confidence. One such spirit was Sir William Barrett, as mentioned above. In one sitting, Feda's voice gave way to a much deeper one as Sir William slowly spoke in the direct-voice (amplified through a cone floating in the air above Mrs. Leonard), stating, with great emphasis: "Life (on his side) is far more wonderful than I can ever tell you, beyond anything I ever hoped for; it exceeds all my expectations."

Drayton Thomas noted various difficulties in communication. "Feda is able on occasion to receive the communicator's thought in a way which produces the effect of a sound," he explained. "At such times, she appears to speak messages verbatim, as if repeating what is dictated to her. This dictation method always reaches a high degree of accuracy, and I realize that I am receiving, not merely the (spirit) communicator's thoughts, but his diction. When, however, Feda receives only the general import of a message and transmits it in her own words the level of accuracy is much lower."

As with other controls, some psychical researchers often wondered if Feda was a secondary personality buried away in Mrs. Leonard's subconscious. Alfred Russel Wallace, co-originator with Charles Darwin of the natural selection theory of evolution, was one the researchers who did not find this a satisfactory explanation. "The conception of such a double personality in each of us, a second-self, which in most cases remains unknown to us all our lives, which is said to have an independent mental life, to have means of acquiring knowledge our normal self does not possess, to exhibit all the characteristics of a distinct individuality with a different character from our own, is surely a conception more ponderously difficult, more truly supernatural than that of a spirit world, composed of beings who have lived and learned, and suffered on earth, and whose mental nature still subsists after its separation from the earthly body," Wallace offered, going on to say that we have to suppose that this second-self, while possessing some knowledge the primary self does not have, either does not know it is part of the whole self or is a persistent liar, as it adopts a distinct name and contends that it once lived a separate life.

Wallace added that he could not conceive how this second-self was developed in us under the law of survival of the fittest, a concept he suggested to Darwin before Darwin went public in 1858 with their parallel theories of evolution.

There are various types of mediumship and they vary considerably. The clairvoyance and/or clairaudience of Lisa Williams differs significantly from the trance voice mediumship and table tilting of Mrs. Leonard. So does the automatic writing form of mediumship involved in Chapters Two and Four.

In her 2000 book, *the Afterlife Codes*, Susy Smith explained her introduction to automatic writing: "Finally, after a long time, a message began to write itself on the paper. It was the most peculiar feeling I'd ever experienced. The hand was just writing by itself without my conscious will being involved in any way. It wrote scragglingly across the page in run-together words."

Smith went on to become one of the best known modern day automatists, eventually moving from the pencil to the typewriter. "Can you imagine how it feels to sit at your typewriter and have your fingers type information that mind does not consciously instigate, that you don't even know?" she offered, going on to explain that her fingers seemed to move of their own volition and what they wrote was as different from what she wanted to say "as popcorn is from peanut butter."

The initial messages purportedly came from her deceased mother, but her mother eventually introduced a new scribe, one who knew much more than she. He was identified as James Anderson, but Smith later discovered that Anderson was a pseudonym for William James, the famous philosopher and psychologist of a century ago. James explained that he used a pseudonym because he was concerned that Smith would have suspected he was a phony if he gave his true identity.

Another fairly recent automatic writer was Grace Rosher of England. In her 1961 book, *Beyond the Horizon*, Rosher explained that she was writing letters to friends one afternoon in 1957 when she heard, apparently clairaudiently, the words, "Leave your hands there and see what happens." To her amazement, the pen started to move without any effort on her part. Words began to form, and the message, "With love from Gordon," slowly appeared. Thus began her regular communication with Gordon Burdick, a long-deceased friend from her youth. Burdick described life on the Other Side and delivered many profound messages.

In the course of time, Rosher was told not to grasp the pen but to simply close her hand in a loose fist and to let the pen rest on top of it. The writing then flowed more fluently. "...I watched the pen move without any conscious effort on my part and write about things I had never dreamed of, and in a style of writing as different from my own as it could possibly be," Rosher wrote.

In the 1918 classic, *The Seven Purposes,* author Margaret Cameron described her sensation in automatic writing as "comparable to that of holding a quiet, live bird, wrapped in a handkerchief, its energy muffled but palpable. Sometimes this sensation of a current from without is communicated to the hand and arm, sometimes only to the fingers."

Probably the most famous and studied case of automatic writing was that of Pearl Curran of St. Louis. First from a friend's Ouija board, then a pencil, then a typewriter, flowed the writings of a person identifying herself as Patience Worth, a 17th Century English woman. In some of her scripts, she used Anglo-Saxon words that are no longer part of the English vocabulary; yet, researchers were able to confirm that these words did exist at one time, although it would have been virtually impossible for Curran, an uneducated 31-year-old woman, to have come upon them.

According to Dr. Walter Franklin Prince, one of the men who studied the phenomena, Patience Worth's writing "displayed original genius, enormous erudition, familiarity with literature and history of many ages, versatility of experience, philosophical depth, piercing wit, moral spirituality, swiftness of thought, and penetrating wisdom," qualities and characteristics which were totally foreign to Pearl Curran. Moreover, Curran was witnessed carrying on simultaneous mental operations as she was recording.

Many automatists, including Smith and Rosher, have questioned whether the subconscious mind was playing tricks on them, as is so often claimed by psychologists. Both wondered how things they had never been exposed to or thought about could come from the subconscious. Smith recognized that her own thoughts and beliefs were sometimes "coloring" the messages and worked diligently to "blank out" her mind.

Rosher consulted a graphologist who compared the handwriting with that in letters received from Burdick when he was alive and concluded that it was indeed the same. Rosher had never heard anything about Burdick's final days and asked him to provide her with some detail. He did and she confirmed the information with mutual friends.

Burdick explained that in order to come into real and tangible contact with Rosher he had to get down to a lower vibration, something which he found very difficult at first but was able to perfect with practice.

William T. Stead, a British journalist who went down with the *Titanic,* was an accomplished automatist. In one of his books, *Letters from Julia,* Stead wrote that he could not believe that any part of his unconscious self would deliberately practice a hoax upon his conscious self about the most serious of all subjects, and keep it up year after year with the most sincerity and consistency. "The simple explanation that my friend who has passed over can use my hand as her own seems much more natural and probable," concluded Stead.

Both Smith and Rosher were warned by their communicators about intruders. "Mother said the misinformation had been written by spirit intruders who were sometimes able to exert more power than she and so could push her aside and take control of the pencil," Smith wrote, further stating that "everyone who dies rebellious is a potential source of mischief." Burdick warned Rosher that there are spirits on his side "who would try to use you in a wrong way."

As mentioned in the Preface, the New Testament's advice to test the spirits to determine if they are of God and to be discerning of the spirits make sense in the light of these warnings.

Perhaps the most accomplished automatist of the 20th Century was Geraldine Cummins (earlier mentioned) of Ireland. In the Introduction of *The Road to Immortality*, published in 1953, Beatrice Gibbes described the method employed by Cummins. She would sit at a table, cover her eyes with her left hand and concentrate on "stillness." She would then fall into a light trance or dream state. Her hand would then begin to write. Usually, her "control" would make some introductory remarks and announce that another entity was waiting to speak. Because of her semi-trance condition and also because of the speed at which the writing would come, Gibbes would sit beside her and remove each sheet of paper as it was filled. Cummins's hand was quickly lifted by Gibbes to the top of the new page, and the writing would continue without break. In one sitting, Gibbes stated, Cummins wrote 2,000 words in 75 minutes, whereas her normal compositions were laboriously put together, perhaps 800 words in seven or eight hours.

Gibbes added that she witnessed the writing of about 50 different personalities, all claiming to be "dead," all differing in character and style, coming through Cummins's hand.

The anonymous spirit communicating with John Scott of England, as documented in Scott's 1948 book, *As One Ghost to Another*, seems to have said much the same thing as Frederic Myers. "I send out my thought to your mind and it fuses with yours, and then you and I produce words together, which you, or rather we, write with your hand," the unseen communicator explained. "There is no way of describing to you with your present knowledge the intricate process of communication."

In the Preface to the book, Scott states that he had previously regarded such things as "a pathetic delusion provoking humour in the daily press and anger in the churches." However, after he had retired to the country, he began experimenting with psychic matters and soon found that in his right hand a "vague urge." When he allowed his muscles to collaborate with the urge, he found his hand scrawling across the paper under it line after line in the semblance of writing. After some experimenting and practice the words became legible and made much sense.

At some point in the discourse, Scott asked his communicator why more spirits do not communicate in such a manner. "There are a few who at first return and communicate through your mediums, but their experience does not encourage them; in fact they soon despair of effecting any notable good," the communicating spirit told him, going on to inform him that it is very difficult to find minds which have the ability to receive such communication.

"I think I may say that most of them become thus absorbed [with their new environment], to the exclusion of all thought of earth," the communicating spirit further told Scott, also mentioning that absolutely no communication comes through without a portion of error, which further frustrates communication.

Scott concluded the Preface of his book with the comment that the product of his hand has been laughed at by family and friends, while doctors have diagnosed him as suffering from a morbid state of schizophrenia. "I have broken into the shadowy abode of the suggested subconscious, seeking 'compensation for frustration' and 'escape,' thus letting loose an actor to simulate two dead persons, one not known to me at all and the other through hearsay," Scott wryly summarized one medical opinion.

"Meanwhile," he ended, "I remain the ordinary human animal of social routine, distinguished from the herd merely by the label."

In an 1889 book titled *Heaven Revised*, author and medium Eliza B. Duffey goes into some of the difficulties of spirit communication. Like Geraldine Cummins, Duffey was an automatic writing medium. "During the entire period in which I was engaged in this writing – some three or four months – I lived and moved in sort of a dream," she explained in the Introduction of the book. "Nothing seemed real to me. Personal troubles did not seem to pain me. I felt as though I had taken a mental anesthetic."

Duffey added that the writing seemed to come through "unseen assistance," though she realized that those who have not experienced it might have a hard time understanding it.

Before Imperator and his "band of 49," including Rector, supplanted George Pellew as Leonora Piper's control, they had worked with William Stainton Moses, who began developing as a medium in 1872, well before Mrs. Piper discovered her own mediumship. However, Imperator functioned more as a teacher for Moses than a go-between. He told Moses that he had come to explain the spirit world, how it is controlled, and the way in which information is conveyed to humans. "Man must judge according to the light of reason that is in him," Imperator voiced through Moses. "That is the ultimate standard, and the progressive soul will receive what the ignorant or prejudiced will reject. God's truth is forced on none."

When a spirit well-known when incarnate communicated with Moses through direct writing, another form of mediumship, in which the writing instrument operates independently of any human hand, his name was spelled incorrectly, leading Moses to suspect an impostor spirit. However, it was explained to Moses by Imperator that the error was by intermediate spirits who were assisting in the communication. The more advanced the spirits, Moses came to understand, the more difficult it was for them to communicate because of the vibratory difference in their levels. Thus, the advanced sprit had to send the message down (in vibration) to lower level spirits to relay it on through or to the medium.

"Most frequently the actual writing is done by one who is accustomed to manifest in that way, and who acts, as it were, as the amanuensis of the spirits who wish to communicate," Imperator informed Moses. "In many cases, several spirits are concerned." In this case, the error was due to inadvertence on the part of one of the intermediary spirits, not the communicator himself."

Apparently, Rector was more involved with Mrs. Piper because he was closer to Piper's lower vibration than was Imperator. That is, Rector was an intermediary between Imperator and Moses.

Moses continually asked for the earthly identifications of Imperator and the others in his group. Imperator initially refused, informing Moses that revealing their earthly names would result in casting additional doubt on the validity of the messages. However, Imperator later revealed their names, advising Moses that they should not be mentioned in the book he would write. It was not until after Moses's death that the identities were made public by A. W. Trethewy in a book, *The Controls of Stainton Moses*. Imperator was Malachias, the Old Testament prophet, while Rector was Hippolytus. Imperator took directions from

Preceptor, who was Elijah. Preceptor, in turn, communed directly with Jesus. Other communicators in the band of 49 included Daniel, Ezekiel, John the Baptist, Solon, Plato, Aristotle, Seneca, Plotinus, Alexander Achillini, Algazzali, Kabbila, Chom, Said, Roophal, and Magus.

It was suggested to Moses by some psychical researchers that all of the messages might have come from his subconscious mind without his being aware of it. But there were so many messages outside of the scope of his education and life experiences as well as in opposition to his beliefs that he simply could not accept such a recondite theory. "Spirits these people call themselves, having an existence independent of my life and consciousness," he wrote in 1889, three years before his death, "and, as such, I accept them."

Likewise, unless one simply does not want to believe in a spirit world, it is difficult to accept Raymond, Bob, Claude, Thomas, and Rolf, the chief communicators in this anthology, as anything other than spirits.

Raymond Lodge

Sir Oliver Lodge

F. W. H. Myers

Gladys Osborne Leonard

CHAPTER ONE

RAYMOND

Background: *Second Lieutenant Raymond Lodge, attached to the South Lancashire Regiment of the Regular British Army, was killed near Ypres, France on September 14, 1915 when struck by a shell fragment in the attack on Hooge Hill.*

The 26-year-old officer was the youngest of six sons born to Sir Oliver Lodge and Lady Mary Lodge. He had been educated at Birmingham University in mechanical engineering and had plans to become a partner with two older brothers in an engineering firm serving the government.

Soon after his death, Raymond began communicating with his parents. The story is set forth in "Raymond or Life and Death," authored by his father and published the following year.

Sir (Dr.) Oliver Lodge had been a professor of physics and mathematics at University College in both London and Liverpool before becoming principal of Birmingham University in 1900. Knighted in 1902 for his scientific work, Lodge was known primarily for his contributions in electricity, thermo-electricity, and thermal-conductivity. He perfected a radio wave detector known as a "coherer" and was the first person to transmit a radio signal, a year before Marconi. He later developed the Lodge spark plug. He was awarded the Rumford Medal in 1898 for his research in radiation, and in 1919 received the Albert Medal of the Royal Society of Arts as a pioneer in wireless telegraphy. He served as president of the prestigious British Association for the Advancement of Science in 1913.

Like so many other scientists caught up in the wake of Darwinism, the senior Lodge had become a materialist, not believing in anything spiritual. However, he remained open-minded on the subject and was intrigued by the idea that one person could read another's mind, something he had observed around 1883 in a stage performer named Irving Bishop. Shortly after witnessing Bishop's performance, he joined the Society for Psychical Research (SPR) and befriended Frederic W. H. Myers, a Cambridge scholar who had co-founded the SPR in 1882.

During the winter of 1889-90, Lodge and Myers closely studied Leonora Piper, an American medium who had been brought to England by the SPR. It was this study of Mrs. Piper that convinced Lodge of the survival of the human personality after death and in spirit communication. "The proof that they retained their individuality, their memory, and their affection, forced itself upon me, as it had done upon many others," Lodge wrote. "So my eyes began to open to the fact that there really was a spiritual world, as well as a material world which hitherto had seemed all sufficient, that the things which appealed to the senses were by no means the whole of existence."

While debunkers of his day and today claim that Lodge was easily duped by charlatans because of his grief over the death of Raymond, it is clear that Lodge came to his conclusions well before Raymond's death. In his 1909 book, "The Survival of Man," he clearly set forth his belief in survival and a spirit world. This book resulted in much shock and disdain among his materialistic colleagues in the scientific community. But Lodge saw no conflict between mainstream science and psychical research. "For myself, I do not believe that physics and psychics are entirely detached," he wrote. "I think there is a link between them; neither is complete without the other. A study of the material world alone may be a narrowing influence. It leaves untouched the whole 'universe of discourse' apprehended by artist, philosopher, and theologian. To emphasize the importance of one part of the universe we need not decry or deny the remainder."

Besides "The Survival of Man" and "Raymond or Life and Death," Lodge authored many books, both on mainstream scientific subjects and psychical research. They included "Man and the Universe" (1908), "Science and Religion" (1914), "Ether and Reality" (1925)," Evolution and Creation" (1926) and "My Philosophy" (1933).

"I tell you with all the strength of conviction which I can muster, that we do persist, that people still continue to take an interest in what is going on, that they know far more about things on this earth than we do,

and are able from time to time to communicate with us," Lodge stated in one of his many speeches. "Communication is possible, but one must obey the laws, first finding out the conditions. I do not say it is easy, but it is possible, and I have conversed with my friends just as I can converse with anyone in the audience now."

Lodge went on to say that he had tried all sorts of other explanations and had eliminated them one by one. "The conclusion is," he said, "that survival of existence is scientifically proved by scientific investigation."

In spite of his high standing in the scientific community, Lodge continually suffered from attacks by scientists grounded in materialism. "I am not going to be unfaithful or to shrink from the responsibility put upon me by being entrusted with knowledge that is now regarded as strange and unprofitable," he responded to his attackers. "No knowledge is really unprofitable, nor is anything in the natural world common or unclean, though it is true that unwise people may make some things appear so...If I can be used by Higher Powers to bear testimony to truth, then, whether palatable or not, that is all I ask. Whatever happens to me, I rejoice in the opportunity of service, and am thankful for the kindly help and guidance forthcoming, though not always recognized at the time. Forward, then, into the Unknown!"

"Raymond or Life And Death,' released a year or so after the death of Raymond, became a best seller and provided comfort to many grieving parents whose children had also died in the war. The "spirit" part of Raymond's story began before Raymond's death with the "Faunus" message, said to be from Frederic Myers, who had died in 1901. As Lodge reported it, Anne Manning Robbins was having a sitting with Leonora Piper in Boston, Massachusetts, USA on August 8, 1915 when she received a message from Richard Hodgson, who had been managing the American branch of the SPR before his death in 1905, to give to Lodge. "Now Lodge, while we are not here as of old, i.e., not quite, we are here enough to take and give messages. Myers says you take the part of the poet, and he will act as Faunus." When Miss Robbins told Hodgson she did not understand the message, he said that Lodge should check with Margaret Verrall, as she would understand. Hodgson added that Arthur said she would understand. This was taken to be Dr. Arthur W. Verrall, Margaret's husband, who also was deceased.

Alta Piper, the daughter of Mrs. Piper, then posted the message to Lodge, it reaching him early September. Lodge didn't understand and wrote to Mrs. Verrall, who like her husband, was an authority on the classics. Mrs. Verrall referred him to a passage in "Horace" in which

Horace gave an account of his narrow escape from death, from a falling tree, as a result of the intervention of the poet Faunus.

Actually, an earlier message came through Mrs. Piper on August 5, while doing automatic writing in a non-trance state. It read: "Yes. For the moment, Lodge, have faith and wisdom in all that is highest and best. Have you all not been profoundly guided and cared for? Can you answer, 'No'? It is by your faith that all is well and has been." This arrived by separate post on the same day as the Faunus message.

Knowing that a fallen or falling tree is a frequent symbol for death because of a misinterpretation of Eccl. xi. 3 in the Old Testament, Lodge wondered if it would be a death in the family or some financial disaster that Myers, his old friend, wanted him to be ready for. It was not until he received a telegram from the War Office informing him of Raymond's death that Lodge understood. He interpreted it to mean that Myers wanted to lighten the blow by letting him know that his son still lives.

Reader alert: *This chapter includes many excerpts from Lodge's 1916 book and a later book, "Raymond Revised." As the dialogue coming through Gladys Osborne Leonard, the entranced medium, can be very confusing, the reader is referred to the more detailed explanation set forth in the Introduction of this book. As pointed out there, Feda, Mrs. Leonard's spirit control, acts as a medium on the Other Side and passes on messages from other spirits, as most of them are unable to communicate directly, at least in the initial stages. Feda often refers to herself in the third person, e.g., "Feda thinks Raymond is trying to say...." and at other times she relates a message as if Raymond is giving it directly. She often changes from a third person statement to a first person statement, within the same message. Her grammar is often imperfect but this shows up only occasionally in the transcripts as those recording the messages were apt to correct them as they recorded them. Lodge apparently left some of the grammatical gaffes in the records as examples.*

Words in standard print are those of Sir Oliver Lodge, while words in italics are those of the editor of this book. Words in indented paragraphs are those coming through the medium from the spirit world. Words in brackets within the indented paragraphs are also those of the editor.

✳ ✳ ✳

The first sitting that was held after Raymond's death by any member of the family was held not explicitly for the purpose of getting into communication with him – still less with any remotest notion of entering into communication with Mr. Myers – but mainly because a French widow lady, who had been kind to our daughters in Paris, was staying with my wife at Edgbaston – her first real visit to England – and was in great distress at the loss of both her beloved sons in the war, within a week of each other, so that she was left desolate. To comfort her, my wife took her to London to call on Mrs. Kennedy, and to get a sitting arranged for with a medium whom that lady knew and recommended. Two anonymous interviews were duly held, and incidentally I may say that the two sons of Madame communicated on both occasions, though with difficulty; that one of them gave his name completely, the other approximately, and that the mother who was new to the subject, was partially consoled. Raymond, however, was represented as coming with them and helping them, and as sending some messages on his own account. I shall here only quote those messages which bear upon the subject of Myers and have any possible connection with the 'Faunus' message.

Report extract: We heard first of Raymond's death on September 17, 1915, and on September 25, his mother (M.F.A.L.), who was having an anonymous sitting for a friend with Mrs. Leonard, then a complete stranger, had the following spelt out by tilts of a table, as purporting to come from Raymond:

> Raymond (through Feda): Tell Father I have met some friends.
> M.F.A.L: Can you give any name?
> Raymond/Feda: Yes, Myers
> (That was all on that subject on that occasion)

On the 27th of September, 1915, I myself went to London and had my first sitting, between noon and one o'clock, with Mrs. Leonard. I went to her home or flat alone, as a complete stranger, for whom an anonymous appointment had been made. Before we began, Mrs. Leonard informed me that her 'control' was a young girl named 'Feda'.

In a short time after the medium had gone into trance, a youth was described in terms which distinctly suggested Raymond and "Feda" brought messages, The "Paul" referred to in them is the deceased son of Dr. and Mrs. Kennedy, he having been asked by his parents privately to help Raymond if he could. Paul had already several times communicated with his mother through Feda. From the record of my sittings I extract the following:

> Feda: There is some one here with a little difficulty: not fully built up; youngish looking; form more like an outline; he has not completely learnt how to build up as yet. Is a young man, rather above the medium height; rather well built. He holds himself up well. He has not been over long. His hair is between colours. He is not easy to describe, because he is not holding himself up so solid as some do... He is not built up quite clearly. but it feels as if Feda knows him. He must have been here waiting for you. Now he looks at Feda and smiles; now he laughs, he is having a joke with Feda, and Paulie laughs too. Paul says he has been here before and that Paul brought him. But Feda sees many hundreds of people, but they tell me that this one has been brought quite lately. Yes, I have seen him before. Feda remembers a letter with him too...
>
> He has been to see you before, and he says that once he thought you knew he was there, and that two or three times he was not quite sure. Feda gets it mostly by impression; it is not always what he says, but what she gets; but Feda says 'he says,' because she gets it from him somehow.
>
> He finds it difficult, he says, but he has got so many kind friends helping him. He didn't think when he waked up first that he was going to be happy, but now he is, and he says he is going to be happier. He knows that as soon as he is a little more ready he has got a great deal of work to do. 'I almost wonder,' he says, 'shall I be fit and able to do it. They tell me I shall.'
>
> I have instructors and teachers with me. Now he is trying to build up a letter of some one: M he shows me. He seems to know what the work is. The first work he will have to do, will be helping at the Front; not the wounded so much, but helping those who are passing over in the war. He knows that when they pass on and wake up, they will still feel a certain fear, and some other word which Feda missed. Feda hears a something and 'fear'. Some even go on fighting; at least they want to; they don't believe they have passed on. So many are wanted, where he is now, to explain to them, and help them, and soothe them. They do not know where they are, nor why they are there.

People think I say I am happy in order to make them happier, but I don't. I have met hundreds of friends. I don't know them all. I have met many who tell me that a little later they will explain why they are helping me. I feel I have got two fathers now. I don't feel I have lost one and got another; I have got both. I have got my old one, and another too – a *pro tem* father.' [Sir Oliver noted that Myers soon afterwards spoke of having practically adopted Raymond.]

There is a weight gone off his mind the last day or two; he feels brighter and lighter and happier altogether, the last few days. There was confusion at first. He could not get his bearings, didn't seem to know where he was. 'But I was not very long,' he says, 'and I think I was very fortunate; it was not very long before it was explained to me where I was.'

Feda feels like a string around her head...a light feeling in the head, and also an empty sort of feeling in the chest, empty as if sort of something gone. A feeling like a sort of vacant feeling there; also a bursting sensation in the head. But he does not know he is giving this. He has not done it on purpose; they have tried to make him forget all that, but Feda gets it back from him. There is a noise with it too, an awful noise and a rushing noise.

He has lost all that now, but he does not seem to know Feda feels it now. 'I feel splendid,' he says. 'I feel splendid! But I was worried at first. I was worried, for I wanted to make it clear to those left behind that I was all right, and that they were not to worry about me.'

He is gone, but Feda sees something which is only symbolic; she sees a cross falling back on to you; very dark, falling on to you; dark and heavy looking; and as it falls it gets twisted round and the other side seems all light, and the light is shining all over you. It is a sort of pale blue, but it is white and quite light when it touches you. Yes, that is what Feda sees. The cross looked dark, and then it suddenly twisted round and became a beautiful light. It is going to help a great deal.... Your son is the cross of light; he is the cross of light, and he is going to be a light that will help you; he is going to help you to prove to the world the Truth. That is why they built up the dark cross that turned to light. You know; but others, they do so want to know. Feda is losing hold; goodbye.

When Lady Lodge was sitting with medium Alfred Vout Peters later that same day, September 27, Raymond communicated with his mother and made reference to a group photo taken 21 days before his death. He mentioned holding a walking stick. Unaware of such a photo, Sir Oliver, in a later sitting with Mrs. Leonard, asked Raymond about the photo and was told that he (Raymond) was sitting down for the photo and that someone behind him was leaning on his shoulder. On December 7, 1915, the Lodges received a copy of the photograph from the mother of another member of Raymond's company. It showed Raymond sitting on the ground with a walking stick over his legs and the officer behind him resting his arm on Raymond's shoulder. (See photo on page 10) Raymond's expression suggests that he was annoyed by the officer behind him resting his arm on his shoulder. Sir Oliver concluded that this evidence went beyond fraud, coincidence and telepathy and saw it as sort of a cross-correspondence in that messages about the photo came through two different mediums. Although Mrs. Leonard was primarily a trance-speaking medium, she also produced table-tilting messages, in which a table would levitate slightly off the ground and then tilt at the proper letter as a sitter recited the alphabet. On September 28, Sir Oliver and Lady Lodge attended a table-tilting session with Mrs. Leonard. Sir Oliver explained:

A table sitting in not good for conversation, but it is useful for getting definite brief answers – such as names and incidents, since it seems to be less interfered with by the mental activity of an intervening medium, and to be rather more direct. But it has difficulties of its own. The tilting of the table need not be regarded as a 'physical phenomenon' in the technical or supernormal sense, yet it does not appear to be done by the muscles of those present. The effort required to tilt the table is slight, and evidentially it must, no doubt, be assumed that so far as mechanical force is concerned, it is exerted by muscular action. But my impression is that the tilting is an incipient physical phenomenon, and that though the energy, of course, comes from the people present, it does not appear to be applied in quite a normal way.

As regards evidence, however, the issue must be limited to intelligent direction of the energy. All that can safely be claimed is that the energy is intelligently directed, and the self-stoppage of the table at the right letter conveys by touch a sort of withholding feeling – a kind of sensation as of inhibition – to those whose hands lie flat on the top of the table. The light was always quite sufficient to see all the hands, and it works quite well in full daylight. The usual method is for the alphabet to be called over, and for the table to tilt or thump at each letter till it stops at the right one. The table tilts three times to indicate "yes," and once to indicate "no"; but as one tilt also represent the letter A of the alphabet, an error of interpretation is occasionally made by the sitters. So also, C might be perhaps be mistaken for "yes,' or *vice versa*, but, that mistake is not so likely.

Unconscious guidance can hardly be excluded, i.e., cannot be excluded with any certainty when the answer is of a kind expected. But first, our desire was rather in the direction of avoiding such control; and second, the stoppages were sometimes at unexpected place; and third, a long succession of letters soon became meaningless, except to the recorder who is writing them down silently, as they are called out to him *seriatim* in another part of the room.

It will also be observed that that at a table sitting it is natural for the sitters to do most of the talking, and that their object is to get definite and not verbose replies.

On this occasion the control of the table seemed to improve as the sitting went on owing presumably to increased practice on the part of the communicator, until towards the end, when there seemed to be some signs of weariness or incipient exhaustion; and, since the sitting lasted an hour and a half, tiredness is in no way surprising.

No further attempt was made to keep our identity from Mrs. Leonard: our name had been given away...

After a wait of four minutes, the table began to tilt. Paul Kennedy identified himself first, there to assist Raymond. When Raymond came through, Sir Oliver tested him by asking him for his nickname. He properly identified his nickname as "Pat." As a further test of identity, Sir Oliver asked him to name of one of his five brothers. The table spelled out N-O-R-M-A- before Sir Oliver interrupted and commented that Raymond was confused. He told him to begin again. The name N-O-E-L was then spelled out, which was one of Raymond's brothers. It was not until Sir Oliver later discussed this with his other sons that it began to make sense. His sons explained to him that 'Norman' was a kind of general nickname used by Raymond when they played hockey together. He would shout: 'Now then, Norman,' or other words of encouragement, to any of his older brothers whom he wished to stimulate. Sir Oliver saw this as evidence against telepathy, since neither he nor Lady Lodge knew of the name. He also saw it as an indication that Raymond, who had discussed psychical research with his father when he was alive, was attempting, perhaps coached by Myers, to provide veridical information by giving a name unknown to his father and mother. As a further test, Sir Oliver asked him for the name of an officer in his unit. The table spelled out "Mitchell," a name unknown to the Lodges but later identified by Sir Oliver as Second Lieutenant E. H. Mitchell.

Sir Oliver pointed out that words came through without a break between them and that when sentences came through they often had to wait for the person recording the letters to make sense of the message.

He added:

Returning to the kind of family records here given, to which evidence is sporadic rather than systematic, though none the less effective, one of the minor points, which yet is of interest, is the appropriate way in which different youths greet their relatives. Thus, while Paul calls his father 'Daddy' and his mother by a pet name, as he used to, and while Raymond calls us simply "Father" and "Mother," as he used to; another youth named Ralph – an athlete who had fallen after splendid service in the war – greets his father, when at length that gentleman was induced to attend a sitting, with the extraordinary salutation "Ullo "Erb," spelt out as one word through the table; though to the astonishment of the medium it was admitted to be consistent and evidential. The ease and freedom of which this Ralph managed to communicate are astonishing, and I am tempted to add as an appendix some records which his family have kindly allowed me to see, but I refrain as they have nothing to do with Raymond.

Raymond is seated in front row, second from right.

On November 17, 1915, Lionel Lodge, one of Raymond's older broth-ers, went to London to sit with Mrs. Leonard, not giving his name or any clue that he was related to the Lodge family. After Mrs. Leonard went into trance, Feda began speaking and said a spirit was coming through whom she knew. "Oh, it's Raymond!" she exclaimed. Reference was made to a table sitting the Lodge family had at their home, one not involving Mrs. Leonard and unknown to her, as well as the fact that Raymond struggled to communicate in that sitting. Lionel asked Raymond what could be done to improve conditions. Feda responded:

He does not understand it sufficiently himself yet. Other spirits get in, not bad spirits, but ones that like to feel they are helping. The peculiar manifestations are not him, and it only confuses him terribly. Part of it was him, but when the table was careening about, it was not him at all. He started it, but something comes along stronger than himself, and he loses the control. [Lionel then asked Raymond about a comment in which Raymond told him that he had a lot to tell him.]

Yes. What he principally wanted to say was about the place he is in. He could not spell it all out – too laborious. He felt rather upset at first. You do not feel so real as people do where he is, and walls appear transparent to him now. The great thing that made him reconciled to his new surroundings was that things appear so solid and substantial. The first idea upon waking up was, he supposes, of what they call 'passing over.' It was only for a second or two, as you would count time [that it seemed a] shadowy vague place, everything vapoury and vague. He had that feeling about it. The first person to meet him was Grandfather. And others then, some of whom he had only heard about. They all appeared to be so solid, that he could scarcely believe that he had passed over.

I live in a house, he says – a house built of bricks – and there are trees and flowers, and the ground is solid. And if you kneel down in the mud, apparently you get your clothes soiled. The thing I don't understand yet is that the night doesn't follow the day here, as it did on the earth plane. It seems to get dark, but the time between light and dark is not always the same. I don't know if you think all this is a bore. [Lionel noted that at this time he was distracted while wondering if his pencil would hold out as he took rapid notes.]

What I am worrying round about is, how it's made, of what it is composed. I have not found out yet, but I've got a theory. It is not an original idea of my own; I was helped to it by words I let drop here and there.

People who think everything is created by thought are wrong. I thought that for a little time that one's thoughts formed the buildings and the flowers, and trees and solid ground, but there is more than that.

[Feda then gives her view of things.] There is something always rising from the earth plane – something chemical in form. As it rises to ours, it goes through various changes and solidifies on our plane. Of course, he is only speaking of where he is now. He feels sure that it is something given off from the earth, that makes the solid trees and flowers, etc. He does not know any more. He is making a study of this, but it takes a good long time.

[Lionel asked if Raymond could contact anyone on earth.] Not always. Only those wishing to see him and who it would be right for him to see. Then he sees them before he has thought. He does not wish to see anybody unless they are going to be brought to him.

He says, I am told that I can meet anyone at any time that I want to; there is no difficulty in the way of it. That is what makes it such a jolly fine place to live in.

[Lionel asked if he can help people still on the earth plane.] That is part of his work, but there are others doing that. The greatest amount of his work is still at the war. He says, I've been home – only likely [lately?]. I've been home—but my actual work is at the war. I have something to do with father, though my work still lies at the war, helping poor chaps literally shot into the spirit world.

[Lionel asked if Raymond could see ahead at all.] I think sometimes that I can, but it's not easy to predict. I don't think that I really know any more than when on earth. [Raymond said he thought Greece had been lost and that he did not agree about Serbia and that Russia would do well all through the winter, and that there would be steady progress all through the winter.] I think there is something looming now. Some of the piffling things I used to be interested in I have forgotten all about.

There is such a lot to be interested in here. I realize the seriousness sometimes of this war....It is like watching a most interesting race or game gradually developing before you. I am doing work in it, which is not so interesting as watching.

[Lionel asked how he might help relative to future attempts at communicating with Raymond.] Just go very easily, only let one person speak, as he said before. It can be H. (Honor) or L.L. (Lionel). Settle on one person to put the questions, the different sound of voices confuses me and I mix it up with questions from another's thoughts. In time I hope it will not so difficult. I wouldn't give it up. I love it. Don't try more than twice a week, perhaps only once a week. Try to keep the same times always, and to the same day if possible. I am going. Give my love to them all. Tell them I am very happy. Very well, and plenty to do, and intensely interested. I did suffer from shock at first, but I am extremely happy now. I'm off.

[Feda now speaking independent of Raymond.] He won't say good-bye. A lady comes too: A girl, about medium height; on the slender side, not thin but slender; face oval shape; blue eyes; lightish brown hair, not golden. [Lionel asks if she can give a name.] She builds up an L. Not like the description when she was on earth. Very little earth life. She is related to you. She has grown up in the spirit life. Oh, she is a sister! [Lionel acknowledged that he had a deceased sister, though no name is given. Sir Oliver later stated that the name was Lily and that she died in infancy. Two other brothers had also died in infancy.] Give her love to them at home, but also principally to Mother. And say that she and her brother, not Raymond, have been also to the sittings at home. She brings lilies with her; she is singing – it's like humming. Feda can't hear the words. She is going now – power is going. [Considering the fact that Lionel went anonymously, Sir Oliver deemed his sitting evidential.]

Lady Lodge sat with Mrs. Leonard on November 26. She began by telling Raymond that they can now face Christmas knowing that Raymond still lives in spirit. Raymond replied that he would be with them at Christmas as long as there is no sadness. If just one sigh, he would "have the hump." Feda expressed confusion, commenting, "hump, what he say?" Lady Lodge asked about his clothes. He replied:

They are all man-u-fac-tured [Feda struggling to pronounce the word]. Can you fancy seeing me in white robes? Mind, I didn't care for them at first, and I wouldn't wear them. Just like a fellow gone to a country where there is a hot climate – an ignorant fellow, not knowing what he is going to; it's just like that. He may make up his mind to wear his own clothes a little while, but he will soon be dressing like the natives. He was allowed to have earth clothes here until he got acclimated; they let him; they didn't force him. I don't think I will ever be able to let the boys see me in white robes. [Much family talk was omitted from the report.]

At a sitting which I had with Mrs. Leonard on December 3, 1915, information was given about the photograph, as already reported. In all these, 'Feda' sittings, the remarks styled *sotto voce* [whispering] represent conversations between Feda and the communicator, not addressed to the sitter at all. I always try to record these scraps when I can overhear them; for they are often interesting, and sometimes better than what is subsequently reported as the result of the brief conversation. For she appears to be uttering under her breath not only her own question or comment but also what she is being told; and sometimes names are in that way mentioned correctly; when afterwards she muddles them. For instance, on one occasion she said sotto voce, 'What you say? Rowland' (in a clear whisper; and then aloud, He says something like Ronald.' Whereas in this case 'Rowland' proved to be correct. The dramatically childlike character of Feda seems to carry with it a certain amount of childish irresponsibility Raymond says that he 'has to talk to her seriously about it sometimes.' [He added that Feda improved over time.]

[Sir Oliver recorded the December 3 sitting, as follows with Feda reporting for Raymond, as usual.] Oh, it is interesting, he says – much more than on the old earth plane. I didn't want to leave you and mother and all of them, but it is interesting. I wish you could come over for one day, and be with me here. There are times you do go there, but you won't remember. They have all been over with him at night time, and so have you, but he thought it very hard you couldn't remember. If you did, he is told (he doesn't know it himself, but he is told this.), the brain would scarcely bear the burden of the double existence, and would be unfitted for its daily duties; so the memory is shut out. That is the explanation given to him...

He keeps on saying something about Alec. He has been trying to get to Alec, to communicate with him; and he couldn't see if he made himself felt – whether he really got through. He thought he had got into a bedroom, and that he knocked, but there wasn't much notice taken....And he also hopes to be able to talk to Lionel with the direct voice; not here, he says, but somewhere else. He is very anxious to speak to him. Through a chap, he says, a direct voice chap.

Well, he says, he wants to try once or twice. He wants to be able to say what he says to Feda in another way. He thinks he could get through in his own home sometime. He would much rather have it there. And he thinks that if he got through once or twice with direct voice, he might be able to do better in his own home. H. (sister Honor) is psychic, he says, but he is afraid of hurting her; he doesn't want to take too much from her. But he really is going to get through. He really has got through at home, but silly spirits wanted to have a game. There was a strange feeling there; he didn't seem to know how much he was doing himself, so he stood aside part of the time.

The direct voice is not the same as the trance voice of Mrs. Leonard. In the direct voice, the spirit communicates through an ectoplasmic larynx and through an amplifier of some kind, called a "trumpet." The voice usually resembles the voice of the person when alive in the flesh. It is a much more rare form of mediumship, though more evidential. Feda continued:

He says he has been trying to go to somebody, and see somebody he used to know. He's not related to them, and the name begins with S. It's a gentleman, he says, and he can't remember, or can't tell Feda his name, but it begins with S. He was trying to get to them, but is not sure that he succeeded. He says it was only curiosity; but he likes to feel that he can look up anybody. But he says, if they take no notice, I shall give up soon, only I just like to see what it feels like to be looking at them from where I am.

He says, my body's very similar to the one I had before. I pinch myself sometimes to see if it's real and it is, but it doesn't seem to hurt as much as when I pinched the flesh body. The internal organs don't seem constituted on the same lines as before. They can't be quite the same. But to all appearances and outwardly, they are the same as before. I can move somewhat more freely, he says. Oh, there's one thing, he says, I have never seen anybody bleed.

[Sir Oliver asked if he has ears and eyes.] Yes, yes, and eyelashes and eyebrows, exactly the same, and a tongue and teeth. He has got a new tooth now in place of another one he had – one that wasn't quite right then. He has got it right...

I knew a man that had lost his arm, but he has got another one. Yes, he has got two arms now. He seemed as if without a limb when first he entered the astral, seemed incomplete, but after a while it grows more and more complete until he got a new one. I am talking of people who have lost a limb for some years.

[Sir Oliver asked about a limb lost in battle.] Oh if they have only just lost it, it makes no difference. It doesn't matter – they are quite all right when they get here. But I am told – he doesn't know this himself, but he has been told – that when anybody's blown to pieces, it takes some time for the spirit body to complete itself, to gather itself all in and to be complete, It dissipated a certain amount of substance which is undoubtedly theri, theric, etheric, etheric, and it has to be concentrated again. The *spirit* isn't blown apart, of course – he doesn't mean that – but it has an effect upon it. He hasn't seen all this, but he has been inquiring because he is interested.

[Sir Oliver asked about bodies that are burnt.] Oh, if they get burnt by accident, if they know about it on this side, they detach the spirit first. What we call a spirit-doctor comes round and helps. But bodies should not be burnt on purpose. We have terrible trouble sometimes over people who are cremated too soon; they shouldn't be. It's a terrible thing; it has worried me. People are so careless. The idea seems to be – hurry up and get them out of the way now that they are dead. Not until seven days, he says. They shouldn't be cremated for seven days.

[Sir Oliver asked what happens if the body goes bad.] When it goes bad, the spirit is already out. If that much (indicating a trifle) of spirit is left in the body, it doesn't start mortifying. It is the action of the spirit on the body that keeps it from mortifying. When you speak about a person 'dying upwards,' it means that the spirit is getting ready and gradually getting out of the body. He saw the other day a man going

16

to be cremated two days after the doctor said he was dead. When his relations on this side heard about it, they brought a certain doctor on our side, and when they saw that the sprit hadn't got really out of the body, they magnetized it, and helped it out. But there was still a cord, and it had to be severed rather quickly, and it gave a little shock to the spirit, like as if you had something amputated; but it had to be done. He believes it has to be done in every case. If the body is to be consumed by fire, it is helped out by spirit doctors. He doesn't mean that a spirit-body comes out of its own body, but an essence comes out of the body – oozes out, he says, and goes into the other body which is being prepared. Oozes, he says, like in a string. String, that's what he says. Then it seems to shape itself, or something meets it and shapes round it. Like as if they met and went together, and formed a duplicate of the body left behind. It's all very interesting.

There are men here and there are women here. I don't think that they stand to each other quite the same as they did on the earth plane, but they seem to have the same feeling to each other, with a different expression of it. There don't seem to be any children born here. People are sent into the physical body to have children on the earth plane. But there is a feeling of love between men and women here which is of a different quality between two men or two women; and husband and wife seem to meet differently from mother and son or father and daughter. He says he doesn't want to eat now. But he sees some who do. He says that they have to be given something that has all the appearances of an earth food. People here try to provide everything that is wanted. A chap came over the other day who would have a cigar. 'That's finished them,' he thought. He means he thought they would never be able to provide that. But there are laboratories over here, and they manufacture all sorts of things in them. Not like you do, out of solid matter, but out of essences, and ethers, and gases. It's not the same as on the earth plane, but they seemed able to manufacture what looked like a cigar. He didn't try one himself, because he didn't care to; you know he wouldn't want to. But the other chap jumped at it. But when he began to smoke it, he didn't think so much of it. He had four altogether, and now he doesn't look at one. They don't seem to get the same satisfaction out of it, so gradually it seems to drop from them. But when they first come they do want things. Some want meat, and some strong drink; they call for whisky sodas. Don't think I'm stretching it when I tell you that they can manufacture even that. But when they have had one or two, they don't seem to want it so much – not those that are near here. He has heard of drunkards who want it for months and years over here, but he hasn't seen any. Those I have seen, he says, don't want it any more – like himself with his suit, he could dispense with it under the new conditions. He wants people to realize that it's just as natural as on the earth plane.

[Sir Oliver asked Raymond if he could provide more evidential information and suggested that he talk it over with Frederic Myers.] I don't know yet. I feel divided between two ways: One is to give you objective proof, such as simple materializations and direct voice, which you can set down and have attested. Or else I should have to give you information about any different experiences here, either something like what I doing now, or through the table, or some other way. But I don't know whether I will be able to do the two things together...

I do want to encourage people to look forward to a life they will certainly have to enter upon, and realize that it is a rational life. All this that I have been giving you now, and that I gave to Lionel, you must sort out, and put in order, because I can only give it scrappily. I want to study things here a lot. Would you think it selfish if I say I wouldn't like to be back now? I wouldn't give this up for anything. Don't think it selfish, or that I want to be away from you all. I have still got you, because I feel you so close, closer even. I wouldn't come back, I wouldn't for anything that anyone could give me...

He says he thinks he was lucky when he passed on because he had so many to meet him. That came, he knows now, through your having been in with this thing for so long. He wants to impress this on those that you will be writing for; that it makes it so much easier for them if they and their friends know about it beforehand. It's awful when they have passed over and won't believe it for weeks – they just think they're dreaming. And they won't realize things at all sometimes. He doesn't mind telling you now that, just at first, when he woke up, he felt a little depression. But it didn't last long. He cast his eyes round, and soon he didn't mind. But it was like finding yourself in a strange place, like a strange city, with people you hadn't seen, or not seen for a long time, round you. Grandfather was with me straight away. And there's some one called Jane comes to him, who calls herself an aunt, he says, Jane. He's uncertain about her. Jane, Jennie. She calls herself an aunt; he is told to call her 'Aunt Jennie.' Is she my Aunt Jennie? he says. [Sir Oliver responded that she was not an aunt, but that his (Raymond's) mother used to call her that.]

It's surprising how many people come up to me, he says, and shake me by the hand, and speak to me. I don't know them from Adam. But they are doing me honour here, and some of them are such fine men. I don't know them, but they all seem to be interested in you, and they say, 'Oh are you his son? How do you do?'

Although Sir Oliver's book about his contacts with Raymond was a best seller in its day and offered comfort to many grieving parents as well as peace of mind to many others, much of the scientific community was aghast that a man of Lodge's standing in that community could be so duped by someone claiming to be a medium. They especially scoffed at the idea that cigars and whisky sodas were available in "heaven." It became a subject of much humor around smoking rooms in England. Sir Oliver wrote:

I am aware that some of the records may appear absurd. Especially absurd will appear the free-and-easy statements about the nature of things 'on the other side' – the kind of assertion which are not only unevidential but unverifiable, and which we usually either discourage or suppress. I have stated elsewhere my own reasons for occasionally encouraging statements of this kind and quoting them as they stand. And though I admit that to publish them is extremely indiscreet, I still think that the evidence, such as it is, ought to be presented as a whole. In particular, I have thought it my duty to cite not only messages likely to contribute to a conviction of permanent existence in another order of being, but also conversations about the conditions and pursuits incidental to the early stages of that other order, in spite of a natural feeling of reticence about statements so strange and unlikely, the truth of which cannot by any ordinary means be tested. I explain in due time and place that we have not as yet the privilege of getting into touch with the complete personality of the departed; we see through a glass darkly, not face to face. But through a more or less turbid medium we do catch glimpses, we do become aware of a real surviving personality. And in order to display the evidence, both in its weakness, it seems fairest to give samples of every kind of thing that is said through a reputable channel; not withholding anything merely because it may affect the judgment of a critic adversely, and not endeavouring to supply adventitious aids in support of a strong case.

The most evidential class of utterance – information about things unknown to anyone present, and also what we call cross-correspondence – is not overlooked; and while every now and then such things occur naturally and spontaneously, sometimes an effort is made to obtain them.

Alec Lodge sat with Mrs. Leonard on December 21, 1915. Raymond began by telling his brother that he had tried to get through to him at home and is getting a little closer to succeeding as he is better able to understand conditions that govern such communication on that side. He explained that he got through, but not satisfactorily, and when he gets so far, he flounders. He added that he was feeling splendid and never thought it possible to feel so well. Alec recorded Feda's words:

He said it is such a solid place, I have not gotten over it. It is wonderfully real. He spoke about a river to his father; he has not seen the sea yet. He has found water, but doesn't know whether he will find a sea. He is making new discoveries every day. So much is new, although of course not to people who have been here some time.

He went into the library with his grandfather – Grandfather William – and also some body called Richard, and he says the book there seem to be the same as you read. Now this is extraordinary. There are books there not yet published on the earth plane. He is told – only told, he does not know if it is correct – that those books will be produced, books like those that are there now; that the matter in them will be impressed on the brain of some man, he supposes an author.

He says that not everybody on his plane is allowed to read those books; they might hurt them – that is the books not published yet. Father is going to write one – not the one on now, but a fresh one.

It is very difficult to get things through. He wants to keep saying how pleased he is to come. There are hundreds of things he will think of after he is gone. He has brought Lily, and William – the young one.

[Alec asked what Raymond sees when he visits at home.] He can't always see more than a corner of the room—it appears vapourish and shadowy. He often comes when you are in bed. He tried to call out loudly: he shouted, but apparently he has not even manufactured a whisper.

As a test of his own, Alec asked Raymond about his favorite music. Alec noted that he then heard Feda questioning Raymond, asking him sotto voce (whispering) "An orange lady?" Still confused, Feda then told Alec that "He says something about an orange lady." Alec felt that this was very evidential as "My Orange Girl" was the last song Raymond bought when "alive." Raymond also mentioned "Irish Eyes," another of his favorites. He also tried to get a third song through, but Feda could get only "M" and "A." Lionel thought it might be "Ma Honey," but at a later sitting at Mariemont, the Lodge estate, Raymond was asked what was meant by the letters M and A, and he was then able to clearly give the name "Maggie Magee," a song unknown to anyone in the family except Norah, his sister, who was not present when the name came through, another indication that telepathy was not a factor in the communication. Alec told Raymond that much of what he had to say seemed to come through altered and very often was affected by the sitter so that people usually get what they expect. Feda replied:

Raymond says, 'I only wish they did!' But in a way you are right. He is never able to give all he wishes. Sometimes only a word, which often must appear quite disconnected. Often the word does not come from his mind; he has no trace of it. Raymond says, for this reason it is a good thing to try, more to come and give something definite at home. When you sit at the table, he feels sure that what he wants to say is influenced by some one at the table. Some one is helping him, some one at the table is guessing at the words. He often starts a word, but somebody finishes it. He asked father to let you come and not say who you were; he says it would have been a bit of fun.

During the November 17 sitting by Lionel Lodge, Raymond informed Lionel that he could tell that Lionel had mediumistc abilities and this would permit him (Raymond) to communicate at home without the assistance of Mrs. Leonard or other mediums. Sometimes during November of 1915, the Lodge family began experimenting at home with the table-tilting form of mediumship. Sir Oliver explained:
After a time some messages were received and family communication without any outside medium have gradually become easy.

Records were at first carefully kept, but I do not report them, because clearly it is difficult to regard anything thus got as evidential. At the same time, the naturalness of the whole, and the ready way in which family jokes were entered into and each new comer recognized and welcomed appropriately, were very striking. A few incidents, moreover, were really of an evidential character, and these must be reported in due course.

But occasionally the table got rather rampageous and had to be quieted down. Sometimes, indeed, both the table and things like flower-pots got broken. After these more violent occasions, Raymond volunteered the explanation, through mediums in London, that he couldn't always control it, and that there was a certain amount of skylarking, not on our side, which he tried to prevent; though in certain of the surprising mechanical demonstrations, and, so to speak, tricks which certainly seemed beyond the normal power of anyone touching the table, he appeared to be decidedly interested, and was represented as desirous of repeating a few of the more remarkable ones for my edification.

I do not, however, propose to report in this book concerning any purely physical phenomena: they require a more thorough treatment. Suffice it to say that the movements were not only intelligent, but were sometimes, though very seldom, such as apparently could not be accomplished by any normal application of muscular force; however, unconsciously such force might be exerted by anyone. It might only be a single person – left in contact with the table.

A family sitting with no medium present is quite different from one held with a professional or indeed any outside medium. Information is freely given about the doing of the family; and the general air is that of a family conversation; because, of course, in fact, no one but the family present.

At any kind of sitting the conversation is rather one-sided, but whereas with a medium the sitter is reticent, and the communicator is left to do nearly all the talking, in a family group the sitters are sometimes voluble; while the ostensible control only occasionally takes the trouble to spell out a sentence, most of his activity consisting in affirmation and negation, a rather effective dumb show.

I am reluctant to print a specimen of these domestic chats, though it seems necessary to give some account of them.

On Christmas Day, 1915, the family had a long table sitting. It was a friendly and jovial meeting, with plenty of old songs

22

interspersed, which Raymond seemed thoroughly to enjoy and, as it were, 'conduct'...

At some of the sittings now, deceased friends, not relatives, were brought by Raymond and gave notable evidence, both to us and to other people, especially the parents in some cases; to widows in others.

At a sitting on January 28, Raymond told his father that he had met the son of an acquaintance of Sir Oliver. He could not get the name across other than it began with an E and that the father's name began with an A and that the father lived in Scotland. E had drowned when his ship sank and had entered the spirit world before Raymond. As near as Sir Oliver could determine, E wanted to contact his father through a medium and was hoping Sir Oliver would contact his father, Dr. A., and persuade him to sit with a medium. With some hesitation, Sir Oliver passed on the message to Dr. A., but he made no mention of any follow-up by Dr. A in the book. Raymond went on to tell his father that he could see that he was often very tired and that he is doing too much. Sir Oliver agreed but said he found it difficult to back off his heavy work schedule. He further recorded:

He says that lots over here talk, and say that you will be doing the most wonderful work of your life through the war. People are ready to listen now. They had too many things before to let them think about them.; but now it's the great thing to think about the after-life.

I want you to know that when first I came over here, I thought it a bit unfair that such a lot of fellows were coming over in the prime of life, coming over here. But now he sees that for every one that came over, dozens of people open their eyes, and want to know where he has gone to. Directly they want to know, they begin to learn something. Some of them never stopped to think seriously before. "He must be somewhere," they say. "He was so full of life, can we find out?" Then I see that through this, people are going to find out, and find out not only for themselves , and will pass it on to many others, and so it will grow.

Raymond says, I am no judge of that, but he isn't the only one that thinks it. He says, I've got a kind of theory, in a crude sort of way, that man has made the earth plane into such a hotbed of materialism and selfishness that man again has to atone by sacrifice of mankind in the prime of their physical life. So that by that prime self-effacement, they will bring more spiritual conditions on to the earth, which will crush the spirit of materialism. He says that isn't how I meant to put it, but I have forgotten how I meant to say it.

Sir Oliver came up with another test by asking Raymond if he knew about "Mr. Jackson." Feda struggled with understanding Raymond's response, but she communicated: "Fine bird...put him on a pedestal." This was especially evidential as Sir Oliver was certain that Mrs. Leonard did not know that Mr. Jackson was the name of Lady Lodge's pet peacock, nor that he had died a week earlier and was in the process of being stuffed and mounted on a wooden pedestal.

On February 4, 1916, Lady Lodge sat alone with Mrs. Leonard and recorded the following:

[Feda speaking]: Raymond is here. He has been all over the place with Paulie, to all sorts of places to the mediums, to try and get poor boys into touch with their mothers. Some are very jealous of those who succeed. They try to get to their mothers, and they can't...they are shut out...They make me feel as though I could cry to one of them. We explain that their mothers and fathers don't know anything about communicating.

He said about someone that she had gone right on to a very high sphere indeed, as near celestial as could possibly be. His sister, he says – can't get her name [presumed to be Lily]. He said William had gone on too, a good way, but not too far to come to him. Those who are fond of you never go too far to come back to you – sometimes too far to communicate, never too far to meet you when you pass over.

[Lady Lodge expressed concern that she might be holding Raymond back.] You gravitate here to the ones you are fond of. Those you are not fond of, if you meet them in the street, you don't bother yourself to say, 'how-do-you do.'

[Lady Lodge expressed surprise that there are streets there.] Yes, He was pleased to see streets and houses. At one time, I thought it might be created by one's thoughts. You gravitate to a place you are fitted for. Mother, there's no judge and jury, you just gravitate, like to like.

I've seen some boys pass on who had nasty ideas and vices. They go to a place I'm very glad I didn't have to go to, but it's not hell exactly. More like reformatory – it's a place where you're given a chance and when you want to look for something better, you're given a chance to have it. They gravitate together but get so bored. Learn to help yourself and immediately you'll be helped. Very like your world, only no unfairness, no injustice – a common law operating for each and every one.

[Lady Lodge asked if all there are of the same rank and grade.] Rank doesn't count as a virtue. High rank comes by being virtuous. Those who have been virtuous have to pass through lower rank to understand things. All go on to the astral first, just for a little.

He doesn't remember being on the astral himself. He thinks where he is now, he is about third. Summerland, Homeland, some call it. It is a very happy medium. The very highest can come to visit you, and yet it is just sufficiently near the earth plane to get to those on earth. He thinks you have the best of it here, so far as he can see.

Mother, I went to a gorgeous place the other day...I was permitted so that I might see what was going on the Highest Sphere. Generally, the High Spirits come to us [Sir Oliver recorded that he was omitting Raymond's description of that High Sphere from the book, because he felt it unwise to relate an experience of a kind which may be imagined, but he continued with Raymond's further discourse with Lady Lodge.]

I felt exalted, purified, lifted up. I was kneeling. I couldn't stand up, I wanted to kneel. Mother, I thrilled from head to foot. He didn't come near me, and I didn't feel I wanted to go near him. Didn't feel I ought. The Voice was like a bell. I can't tell you what he was dressed or robed in. All seemed a mixture of shining colours.

No good; can you imagine what I felt like when he put those beautiful rays on to me? I don't know what I've ever done that I should have been given that wonderful experience. I never thought of such a thing being possible, not at any rate for years, and years, and years. No one could tell what I felt, I can't explain it.

[Lady Lodge asked if others will understand it.] I know father and you will, but I want the others to try. I can't put it into words. I didn't walk, I had to be taken back to Summerland, I don't know what happened to me. If you could faint with delight. Weren't those beautiful words?

I've asked if Christ will go and be seen by everybody; but was told, 'Not quite in the same sense as you saw Him'. I was told Christ was always in spirit on earth – a sort of projection, something like those rays, something of him in every one. People think he is a Spirit, walking about in a particular place. Christ is everywhere, not as a personality. There is a Christ, and he lives on the highest plane, and that is the one I was permitted to see.

There was more given to me in that beautiful message. I can't remember it all. He said the whole of it, nearly and word for word, of what I've given you. You see from that, I'm given a mission to do, helping near the earth plane...

Mr. Myers was very pleased. He says, you know it isn't always the parson, not always the parson that go highest first. It isn't what you professed. It's what you've done. If you have not believed definitely in life after death, but have tried to as much as you could, and led a decent life, and have left alone things you don't understand, that's all that is required of you. Considering how simple it is you'd think everybody would have done it but very few do....

Some people asked me, are you pleased with where your body lies? I tell them I don't care a bit. I've no curiosity about my body now. It's like an old coat that I've done with, and hope some one will dispose of it. I don't want flowers on my body. Flowers in house, in Raymond's home. Power is going, good night.

On March 3, 1916, Sir Oliver had a sitting with a Mrs. Clegg, an elderly medium. It was arranged by Katharine Kennedy, the mother of Paul, Raymond's friend in spirit, as she apparently had had good results with Mrs. Clegg, whose mediumship did not require a control on the other side, like Feda, i.e., the communicating spirit would directly control Mrs. Clegg. However, even though Raymond purportedly said a few words, the sitting was for the most part a failure. Later that day, Sir Oliver again sat with Mrs. Leonard. Raymond communicated and said he had been at Paul's house and wanted to speak through Mrs. Clegg, but he found it very difficult as one feels very strange when trying to control the medium, i.e., it was much easier when someone like Feda was acting as control on his side. He explained that Paul was able to communicate through Mrs. Clegg with his mother, but it involved some practice, and he (Raymond) apparently needed more practice. He said that he felt he was getting control of Mrs. Clegg, but when he tried to speak he lost his bearings. Sir Oliver found Raymond's description of conditions at the Kennedy home, including his comment that Mrs. Clegg "flopped around" after going into trance, accurate and somewhat evidential.

On May 26, 1916, Lionel Lodge and his sister, Norah, drove from the Lodge home, near Birmingham, to London for a sitting with Mrs. Leonard. Knowing that his brother and sister were scheduled to meet with Mrs. Leonard at noon, Alec Lodge asked two other sisters, Honor and Rosalynde, to sit with him in the drawing room and focus on asking Raymond to get the word "Honolulu" through to Lionel and Norah during the sitting. Lionel and Norah knew nothing of this request.

When Sir Oliver later read Lionel's notes of the sitting, he saw that Raymond said something about Norah playing music. Norah replied that she could not. Feda then whispered to the invisible Raymond (attention directed away from Lionel and Norah), "She can't do what?" Upon getting a response from Raymond, Feda then said, "He wanted to know whether you could play Hulu – Honolulu. Well, can't you try to? He is rolling with laughter."

By the end of May 1916, a preponderance of evidence – if not evidence beyond a reasonable doubt – that Raymond had been communicating with them had been accumulated by the Lodge family. "The number of more or less convincing proofs which we have obtained is by this time very great," Sir Oliver wrote, adding that some of them appeal more to one person, some to another; but taking them all together every possible ground of suspicion or doubt seemed to the family to be removed.

Sir Oliver's book, "Raymond or Life And Death," went to the publisher around June 1, 1916 and was released around October 1 of that year. "Raymond Revised," a more condensed version of the original 404-page book, was released five years later and included some additional contacts with Raymond, including a sitting Lady Lodge and daughter Honor had on January 23, 1917 with Mrs. Robert Johnson, a direct-voice medium. They observed a trumpet floating around the room, held by unseen hands, usually stopping in front of the person to whom the communication was directed. Honor Lodge recorded that after the trumpet *stopped in front of others and they received communication it came to her and her mother. They both heard Raymond's voice as they remembered it when he was still in the earth realm, but he struggled to communicate, saying only that they should tell Father they heard from him and that "I am always with you." The trumpet then stroked both Lady Lodge and Honor before floating on to another person.*

Three weeks later, on February 12, Sir Oliver and Lady Lodge sat with Mrs. Leonard, Raymond talked about his mostly failed efforts to communicate through the trumpet.

I was there, but I was a little disappointed because I couldn't get hold of the power, felt as if I couldn't manage things properly. But I hope I can do better another time. Somebody was there and spoke to me, but I couldn't see clearly, there was a sort of fog around. Somebody tried to help me too much, somebody I didn't know.

He's showing Feda a sitting room, and a room in your house, some other room. It wasn't yesterday or today. He thinks several people were there, not just you alone, he's going back a little...

[Lady Lodge mentioned that she heard his voice.] He's glad of that. But he was rather disappointed at the time, for he couldn't get the power and keep it. He got it and then it dissipated. He couldn't think of tests while he was there. He's keen on tests and had saved some to say, but he couldn't say them. He could say nothing but generalities. He says he touched you too, he thinks he touched you twice.

[Lady Lodge confirmed this.] It was a pleasure to him. He wants to know, did the voice sound like mine, Mother? Somebody was helping me too much. Somebody on the other side, he says, was trying to help him. They tried to make him raise his voice, and when he did that, he got a funny sound, something he couldn't recognize. And it disappointed him rather. He thought he did better when he talked more gently. He felt inclined to say, 'ah weel.' [Sir Oliver interpreted this to mean that Raymond was influenced to speak broad Scotch because one of Mrs. Johnson's controls, David Duguid, speaks that way.]

Yes, I felt like saying 'ah weel,' but fortunately I was able to refrain. Mother, I got very near it...The intonation was better when it was low. They tried to help, and it disconcerted me.

To tell the truth, I couldn't see properly. I thought it was one of the girls with you. I sensed some one else. I felt I ought to know, one of the family, but it was only sensing. I couldn't see them.

Sir Oliver concluded that this was a very evidential sitting, since Mrs. Leonard had no knowledge of the Johnson sitting, although he realized that the debunkers would probably say that Mrs. Johnson must have known Mrs. Leonard and passed on the information about the sitting with her.

On March 24, 1917, in a sitting with Mrs. Leonard, Sir Oliver communicated with Frederic Myers. He asked Myers why he can't get something through that is of a scientific nature, something new and important. Myers replied:

The scientific people, I fear, find it more difficult (he's smiling when he says this) to communicate freely or forcibly, through the extremely limited methods at present in our hands, than those who had developed in other ways.

It's more difficult to get hard facts through than poetical and simpler or literary utterances. Those appear to come freely, like riding on the top of a wave (moving hand sinuously). But to hammer hard scientific fact through I fear, would be difficult; and if we start we ought to devise new means or methods (Feda can't get that.) Well, I'll put it more simply. We may have to devise some means, or a code for understanding each other. So that it can be given through mediums to whom the scientific terms would [not?] present great difficulties. Taking the brains of a medium as a sieve, few have sieves such that we can put through it particles too large for the mesh. The medium would not absorb and transmit without great difficulty.

After Myers communicated, Raymond came through and further discussed the difficulties in communication, mentioning that he was aware that he had contradicted himself on two occasions. Sir Oliver replied that he was aware of them and considered that it was not Raymond communicating. Raymond went on to explain (paraphrased by Sir Oliver for brevity purposes):

Other conditions may not have been right. A medium's guides often impress themselves, and then there's a mixture. Even when I'm there, they get mixed in. I've been trying new ways of getting through; speaking is one, but the voice is not like mine; I haven't got a double-bass voice, and yet there are tones of mine in it. I could do better if they would let me alone. The guides are too kind. I don't speak American, do I? [Lady Lodge confirmed that he didn't speak American.]

I see you sometimes. When there's a good deal of power I get the physical in sight. Dark seems to help me to see. I also occasionally go to sittings when some one is present who has been impressed by our book – I usually call it my book, but I'll stretch a point and call it 'our' book – When I know that and their thoughts reach me, I go and send a little word to them.

Sir Oliver again put another test to Raymond, asking him if he remembered a certain name, giving no other clue. Raymond immediately identified him as a former servant in the Lodge household and recalled his "peculiarities." Raymond said that he was aware that this man had called on Sir Oliver recently and that Sir Oliver had given him some money to help him out.

The number of incidents that show his awareness of what the family is doing, and of their illnesses and difficulties and successes, their anxieties and joys and sorrows is legion. I must just make the assertion that he frequently shows how closely he continues in touch with us, and leave it there.

Finally, I will take a non-evidential passage or two from communication received in 1918.

He chaffed his mother about a mistake of a day in what was evidently meant for his memorial tablet which had been put up at St. George's Church, Edgbaston; saying through Feda, that a Wednesday had been put for a Tuesday (which was true – so that the day of the month does not correspond with the day of the week), that it didn't worry him; he was rather amused.

At the same sitting, which was with Mrs. Leonard, at Datchet, on April 21, 1918, after speaking about several people for evidential reasons, he gave another of those unverifiable descriptions of things on the other side, about which we hadn't heard so much lately. His mother had taken a stenographer with her, so the record of what Feda reported him as saying is more complete than usual; and with that I will conclude this over-long chapter.

Here is the record for what it may be worth of this portion of a long sitting in which he had talked usefully about many people until his mother interrupted [and asked him to tell more about his life].

What he liked more than anything is going to the different spheres. He does like that. And you remember his telling you once about an experience he had had? He's been [back] there many times since. Many, many, many times.

[Lady Lodge asked if he gets there more easily now.] That is what Raymond says: - I told you the first time I couldn't collect my thoughts at all. The second time was better, and I felt I had more command over myself. I knew more what to expect. But strangely enough, the third time I had become rather too confident, and I felt almost as bad as the first time. To go there, one must be prepared, and almost hold oneself in a state of awe, and must not feel too confident in one's ability to stand things. I received such a lot of teaching there. Teaching.

He says he's learnt so much he couldn't find words to tell you about it through a medium. It's made everything on the earth plane, about religion, right and wrong, about choosing between right and wrong, clear, made it all so clear. He often thinks that if he could come back he could fly through life. And he believes that if only people would go within themselves, more, just now and again, that they would reach out and get a good deal of what he has learnt. But when they want to do things on the earth plane, they don't wish to go within themselves, because they are so afraid of reaching a decision against what they wish to do. That is the reason people can't choose between right and wrong.

He's met a lot of friends of his that have been to the same sphere, and it's wonderful how they look at it from different points of view. Some think one thing, some another. He says he's quite sure that when He speaks to them, it is as Raymond thought at first. He doesn't speak in words to them, but soul to soul, or mind to mind. If it were words, why should a thousand of us all get a different message at once? But it must be His Soul and Mind so wonderfully developed.

He says, I know people try to prove that there are other great teachers; and there may have been; but when you get into the spirit world, you will understand why there is no one like Him, no one.

He was taken one day to the – he might say – he doesn't know how to put this into words because he doesn't think any words could picture it. You remember how he told you that he went up through the spheres and got in the seventh sphere. How he told you he went up an opening through the fourth and fifth and sixth spheres, and how different the atmosphere was on the seventh, and how at first he couldn't stand it. As if he wasn't sure of himself, lost command over himself. He heard people on the earth plane speak about getting into a different dimension. Well, it almost felt like that, as if everything was upside down.

He asked, if that is the seventh sphere, what is there beyond it? And they told him, "God only". And he said, What do you mean by "God only"? You see he says, I wanted to know wasn't Jesus God, or what we might call the embodiment of God. And they said, As you were taught on the earth plane, he is the Son of God, and the Spirit of God is within Him; not all God, but such of God as he can contain. That is why He called Himself Son of God, not God Himself. I wanted to get the psychical sense of it, I was so anxious to; and they told me I could not go immediately, but must attend special lectures before I could go to see. Very few could go, they said.

But when I went to the lectures on my own sphere, I found that certain material knowledge, and mechanical things, that I had taken an interest in when there, helped me to understand what I was going to see outside the sphere. The boys will understand one part of this and not the other.

So they took me past the seventh sphere next time. They didn't stop at the seventh sphere, they went on, as if still going up in the opening, and told me to concentrate and to think of myself as a mind, not even as a spirit body. To try to do that. And the more I tried to it, the easier it became to think of myself almost as a germ.

Why can't I be myself? I asked. They said, 'No, don't ask questions, think of yourself as something small. Mind only, power of perception only.' In fact, they said I was to try and think of myself as an egg! I don't know why an egg came easier, but directly I did that. I began to feel that flight, that movement was easier. And I got on to the – I don't know what to call it—I got on to what might be called a corner, like Land's End in England. Yes, a corner, like Land's End in England. Now it is no wonder that they said to think of myself as small, because I felt it was a wonder that I wasn't blown north, south, east, and west, at once. The air seemed as if it was nothing more or less than electric rivers, as if I were in a river. A river of electricity or force going all ways at once. One second it flowed going that way, the next second that way.

My feelings were extraordinary; it didn't worry me, but again I got that great clarity of vision that I told you I had before on the seventh, in the presence of Jesus. This was in the presence of something that my mind could not grip, but my soul saw and understood that I was in the presence of infinity. It had no form; it has no size. It was neither hot nor cold. There was nothing that our finite minds can grasp. I knew it while there, but not now.

A guide was with me – I don't know if I told you that – and the guide said, 'Keep small'; and I knew I had to contract again. I didn't say to him, What is this force? But he kept understanding questions without my asking them.

He said, – You are in the presence of the Infinite. What you feel is the Life-Force that goes from God through all the spheres, and feeds the earth plane. Without this, there would not be a person physically alive on the face of the globe. Not an animal, plant or flower. without this Force that you can feel now.

I felt – not disappointment – but I wished It was something I could define, some shape. The guide said – 'Don't you understand that things only take finite shape on the earth plane, so that your infinite minds can grasp a little bit of what belongs to this; and perhaps in time to come, much more of it will be in you. But it is something beyond yourself. It's the Infinite. Therefore you can't grasp it.

My mind didn't grasp it, but my soul did and the guide said to me, without any asking. Your soul grasps it because your soul belongs to it. It is only with your soul that you can understand this. The mind need not worry about shapes and forms. Let your soul grow up to it, and your mind will follow by degrees. Oh, I can't tell you!

[Lady Lodge asked if the Power is all powerful and if there is any evil fighting it.] Mother, we all know here, any intelligent spirit knows, that the only evil is on the earth plane, and on the lower planes, the astral ones.

The Infinite Good is fighting evil on the earth plane and on the astral. And the Infinite Good must conquer. Evil persists on the earth plane because it belongs there. It is the lower physical selves of man who have created this evil, and the more their souls become uppermost in their make-up, the more they will help themselves. This Force is to assist them. It is going to conquer, but it would not be right for it to crush evil by a miracle. Man couldn't learn. If man doesn't see the fight, he won't see the importance of developing the Good in the physical.

That is the reason the War has been going on so long. If it had stopped after a few months, man would have been ready for evil again – England would have been ready again in two years – any country would have been.

England has learnt a spiritual lesson that she will never forget. Father knows, and will know more. You and I and Father could not have done what we have done if it had not been for the war. The war is a lever that is pressing upon the door between the two worlds, battering down the evil and letting in the good. It seems awful, but if you only saw what I have seen, you would know that evil is only a little spot on a great white surface.

Feda: He's losing the power. That's only one of the things; he's learnt a lot about it. He wouldn't say he would be often able to go, but he is taught a lot about that Force and about how it is employed. It is just as real a force as electricity; tell Father.

Sir Oliver concluded "Raymond Revised" by saying that the primary object of the original book was to bring comfort to those bereaved by the war, and there was no doubt in his mind, based on the favorable feedback he had received, that the book had brought solace and peace of mind to many. At the same time he cautioned that mediumship is not for everyone and stressed that there were many charlatans posing as genuine mediums. As for continuing contacts with Raymond, he wrote:
Concerning the particular case of my son Raymond, I have had many further talks with him, but the stress and anxiety to communicate has subsided. The wish to give scientific evidence remains, but, now that the fact of survival and happy employment is established, the

communication is placid – like an occasional letter home. He has, however, been successful in bringing to their parents a number of youths whom he knew before death, and the weight of evidence has accordingly heavily increased...

One difficulty which good people feel about allowing themselves to take comfort from the evidence, is the attitude of the Church to it, and the fear that we are encroaching on dangerous and forbidden ground. I have no wish to shirk the ecclesiastical point of view; it is indeed important, for the Church has great influence. But I must claim that Science can pay no attention to ecclesiastical notice-boards; we must examine wherever we can, and I do not agree that any region of inquiry can legitimately be barred out by authority.

Occasionally the accusation is made that the phenomena we encounter are the work of devils; and we are challenged to say how we know that they are not of evil character. To that the only answer is the ancient one—"by their fruits..." I will not elaborate on it: St. Paul gave a long list of the fruit of the Spirit in *Galatians v* 22-23. Yet, I do not mean to say that no precautions need be taken and that everything connected with the subject is wholly good: I do not regard as wholly good any activity of man. Even the pursuit of Science can be prostituted to evil, as we now see too clearly in the war. Everything human can be used and abused. I have to speak in platitudes to answer these objections; they are often quite unworthy of the sacred name of religion; they savour of professionalism. Chief Priests were always ready to attribute anything done without their sanction to the power of Beelzebub. The Bishop of Beanvais denounced Joan of Arc's voices as diabolical. It is a very ancient accusation. In the light of historical instances, it is an over-flattering one: I wish to give no other answer...

Meanwhile [our deceased children] are happier and more at home in Paradise. There they find themselves still in touch with earth, not really separated from those left behind, still able actively to help and serve. There is nothing supine about the rest and joy into which they have entered. Under the impact of their young energy, strengthened by the love which rises toward them like a blessing, the traditional barrier between the two states is suffering violence; is being taken by force. A band of eager workers is constructing a bridge, opening a way for us across the chasm; communication is already easier and more frequent than ever before; and in the long run we may feel assured that all this present suffering and bereavement will have a beneficent outcome for humanity.

So may it be!

CHAPTER TWO

BOB

Background: *A heartwarming movie titled "A Rumor of Angels" was released in 2002 and is occasionally seen on television reruns. The film stars Vanessa Redgrave as an elderly recluse in a small ocean-front town. She befriends a 12-year-old neighbor boy who is grieving the loss of his mother in an auto accident. She tells the boy about how her son had communicated with her following his death in the Vietnam War during 1974 and gives the boy her diary of spirit communication from her son. The boy reads various entries in the diary and finds comfort in them until his stepmother and father discover the diary and conclude that the boy's mind is being poisoned by the elderly woman and prohibit him from further visiting her. When the elderly woman dies, she communicates with the boy from the Other Side.*

Probably few people who have viewed the movie realize that it was purported to be based on a true story, although it took place in World War I, not the Vietnam War. The story, with many Hollywood modifications, came from the 1918 non-fiction book,"Thy Son Liveth: Messages from a Soldier to his Mother," by Grace Duffie Boylan. The book was initially released anonymously, but later issues carried Boylan's name. It was not stated that Boylan was the mother of Bob, the young soldier about whom the story revolves, but that seems to have been the implication, though one might infer that Boylan recorded the story as related to her by another person. When the publisher, Little Brown and Company, questioned Boylan as to the authenticity of the story, she replied, "I ask you to regard this book as truth, unaccompanied by proofs of any sort, making its own explanation and appeal."

Boylan, a respected journalist, was married four times – to George Roe, Robert Boylan, St. George Kempson, and Louis Geldert. Speculation is that Bob, given the surname "Bennett" in the book, was Bob Boylan, the son of Robert Boylan. He was said to have grown up with his widowed mother in an old home on the Hudson, below Tarrytown, New York. He went to Columbia University, where he studied electrical engineering, and soon after joining the United States Army was commissioned as a second lieutenant and sent off to fight in World War I. Well before he went to college, Bob developed an interest in telegraphy and set up a wireless in his home with a large mast on the roof.

Reader Alert: *The words below in standard print are those of Boylan, verbatim from the book, with abridgements. Words in italics are those of the editor of this book, while indented words in standard print are those of Bob. For reference purposes, the presumption is that Boylan was Bobs' mother.*

✳✳✳

Bob took to telegraphy as a spark takes to the air wave. He was one of the first to raise a wireless mast from the top of his home, and of course, I had to study and experiment with him. He bullied me into learning the code and being the party of the second part to take his messages. Looking back upon this now, I am impressed with the methods that are used by the Destiny that shapes our ends. Had it not been for that inkling of the science of telegraphy which I gained in our play, I should not have heard a message that – but I will speak of this further.

It was something of a bore to me to put in my time trying to master a complex thing like the wireless; and, of course, I never did become proficient. But when the grind was over, and we both had acquired some speed and receptiveness, it was great fun; and we had a secret between us that made us pals. We used to sit up here in this room and pick up diplomatic secrets, which we could not, fortunately, decode, and international messages which we could not, unfortunately, I believe now, decipher. And when Bob began to really grapple with the mathematics which were to make his path straight to his eagerly adopted profession of electrical engineering, he spent his leisure hours in trying to simplify Marconi's already simple apparatus.

At some point in those years when Bob was still living at home, he received an official order from Washington, D.C. ordering him to dismantle his instrument. Bob protested to the government, but to no avail. Although he complied with the order, he left the receiver where it was.

"Thunderation, mother," he said. "I can't get away from the feeling that I ought to get up to the nth degree in this science! The Germans are using it in ways that we do not know. And if I am called to fight, as of course I shall be, I want a trick up my sleeve that will beat the enemy at his own game. Anybody but you would laugh to hear me say it; but I have a hunch that I am going to be needed in some particular capacity before we win this war. And you mark my words; some day when you are up here in this old room of mine, you are going to hear from your little Robbie...

I did not think it possible then. But I remembered what he had said when the old house was only a lonely, gray pile of empty rooms and he had gone, with the unit, at the first call to arms.

What I felt to see my only son go to war is just what other mothers have felt and will feel as more and more young men are given to their country. But what further I have to reveal is what every father and mother should know. And quite simply I am going to tell it.

Bob was assigned to an Engineers' Corps and soon won his commission as second lieutenant. He was among the first to cross. I had a dozen letters from "Somewhere in France," and it was not hard to catch something of his spirit and enthusiasm. He was glorying in his hard work and his prospects for getting a whack at the Hun. He had qualified for wireless work, much to his delight, and had been out on a reconnaissance. Pershing, himself, had commended him. He warned me not to worry if I did not often hear – that letters are hard to get through. And now came one telling me of fun in camp and the brighter side of soldering. He added that I had been a brick to him and made him a man.

I brought this letter up to read in his room and was laughing and crying over it, as women will, when the wireless signaled "attention." I sprang to the key, and in a moment I had the message that Bob had promised to find means to send me here. It is before me now as I make the translation from the Morse code, adding only the marks of punctuation...

Mother, be game. I am alive and loving you. But my body is with thousands of other mothers' boys near Lens. Get this fact to others if you can. It's awful for us when you grieve, and we can't get in touch with you to tell you we are all right. This is a clumsy way. I'll figure out something easier. I'm confused yet. Bob.

So the news that my son had been killed came to me from his own intelligence by the methods we had used together in our experiments here in this very room. And as I am transcribing it, as he told me to do, for all to see who can be convinced of its sincerity. I have no explanation or proofs other than those that are given here. A man who was killed in battle and is yet alive, and able to communicate with the one closest to him in sympathy, must make his own arguments. I have no knowledge of established psychic laws or limitations. But I know what I know.

A month later, official notice of Bob's death on the battlefield was received by Boylan. She concluded that Bob's first wireless message to her came not long after he fell. Before then, however, the mother had already received several additional wireless messages. In the second one, Bob communicated:

Attention! Get this across – there is no horror in death. I was one minute in the thick of things, with my company, and the next minute Lieutenant Wells touched my arm and said: 'Our command has crossed: Let's go.' I thought he meant the river, and followed him under the crossfire barrage the Tommies made, up to a hillside that I had not noticed before: a clean spot and not blackened by the guns. Lots of fellows I knew were there, and strange troops. But they looked queer. I glanced down at myself. I was olive drab, all right. But my uniform was not khaki. It seemed to be a fabric of some more tenuous kind. I had no gun. I overtook Wells. 'What in the deuce is the matter with me, with us all?' I asked. He said, 'Bob, we're dead.' I didn't believe it at first. I felt all right. But the men were moving, and I fell in line. When we marched through the German barbed-wire barricades and in front of the howitzers, I realized that the body that could be hurt had been shed on the red field. Then I thought of you. Sent the wireless from an enemy station in the field. The officer in charge couldn't have seen me. But he heard, I guess, by the way his eyes popped. He sent a few shots in my direction, anyway. I am using an abandoned apparatus in a trench today, depending on relays. We are assigned to duty here for the present according to Wells. I don't know how he knows. It seems while we have no supernatural power to divert or stop bullets, we can comfort and reassure those who are about to join us. There has been much talk about the presence of one supposed to be the Savior among the dying. I should not wonder if that were true. The capacity for believing is enlarged by experience. But as yet I have no more real knowledge than any of the other fellows. I will let you know as I gain information. Others, like me, will pick up and relay the messages.

Boylan faithfully recorded her son's messages, inserting the proper punctuation and apparently adding some missing words to provide the necessary flow in otherwise truncated verbiage. In the third message, Bob communicated:

Attention! As I see this war, a curious understanding of its purpose and ultimate result is dawning in my mind. The soldiers are the pick of humanity. The young, brave, blameless manhood that has been brought to its majority on the earth so that it may form an ideal democracy in this existence which, I am told, is of permanent character. I am bungling the big idea. But, you know what I mean, mother. I'll grow clearer, maybe. Wells is getting to be a whale of an oracle. Some of the fellows are in a funk, and others are sullen and unhappy, homesick, I guess. The young married men, mostly. If they could get in touch with their folks, it would be all right. That's why I want to try and simplify some system of communication. You have never failed me; and now if you can get it firmly fixed in your mind that I am I, not what is vulgarly called a ghost but a being just as much as I ever was, we can start something worth while. It's got to begin with someone as level-headed as you are. I'm called away.

In the fourth wireless message, Bob encouraged his mother to attempt automatic writing, as it was too difficult trying to get through on a wireless. She confessed ignorance of such "occult" practices, admitting that she had always turned away from books of alleged spiritual sources because the "author souls" seemed so unadvanced intellectually, whereas she expected an all-wise, all-seeing, all-knowing angelhood. However, considering Bob's initial state of confusion, she was by this time beginning to realize that newly-departed souls are somewhat the same as when they leave the earth plane. It was at this time that Bob suggested that his mother compile a book of the messages in order to get the word out to grieving parents that their sons are still "alive."

It may require practice, but I am told there is no reason in the worlds, — notice the plural, — why we should not talk with the greatest ease and without any mechanics. Come up and try tomorrow. See if I can't project my thought direct to yours. Bring pencil and tablet if you want to. But a fellow here who knows all about automatic writing says there is no pencil-guiding by unseen hands about it. The recipient just takes dictation. Better bring the pencil. You will want to report this just as it is for our purposes. I'll find out all I can, but just now we are engaged here in relief work. Some of the chaps are very young, and we see them through. I'll explain about those unusual faculties when I learn more definitely about them.

Boylan's initial attempts at automatic writing were failures. She felt that she was "faking" the messages. She continued practicing and finally got a few words, then some sentences. Bob further advised her.

Get into a quiet corner and listen with your inner ear. Your unused finer perceptions. You will be able to really hear what I am saying, after some practice. I am told this by a man who has come to instruct us. I think, on my own hook, that you will have to rid your mind of worry or prejudice before we can make much headway. Any one who wants to can put out a mental wire that will be picked up. But you must 'be aware of strangers!' Quote that. There are scalawags ready to jump into all conversations and mix up things if they are permitted to do so. Keep your wires clear.

You ask how to keep the scalawags away — and who and what are they? I don't just know who they are. I'll try and find out. But you have to 'make a law.' That sounds occult and I do not want anything to be spooky or unnatural in these letters. But that is the expression I hear often concerning this particular difficulty. These wire tappers cannot get by, it seems, unless you permit them to fool you. You say: 'I will not entertain mischievous spirits' – or something like that; and they beat it. I do not know why that is efficacious. But it is.

Bob went on to tell his mother that he could see her mind like a white screen, and that he knew he could write on it. He continued to advise her in perfecting the automatic writing and it began to flow.

Don't try to hold your pencil any differently than you hold it ordinarily, mother, dear, I am not guiding your pencil. As I figure it out, I am simply dictating these letters by some improved form of telepathy, to your mind. You do the writing. It is wholly simple. I really talk and you hear... We all have perceptions and faculties that are capable of lifting us into supermen. The rub is we do not suspect our own powers. Do not let yourself be led into a maze of reasons why this thing cannot be. What is, is.

The automatic writing was now coming through regularly and the telegraphic messages ceased. Bob explained that he was still adjusting to his new conditions and there were about a thousand men at what he could only refer to as "field headquarters." He likened his work to Red Cross units, working to relieve suffering among the wounded and guiding newcomers into the afterlife environment.

Mother, the soul leaves the body as a boy jumps out of a school door. That is, suddenly and with joy. But there is a period of confusion when a fellow needs a friend. Quote that. We are the friends. I guess that is the best explanation I can give. I told you Jack Wells came through with me. He has gone away now. I am told we go to other departments of usefulness, as others, suited to this field work, come on here. I will tell you as much as I can.

You complain that you cannot really get much of an idea of conditions here from what I tell you. I want you to be able to take my dictation like a prize-winner, and in the meantime, I'll try and get a line on things here. So far it is nothing very different from what we knew before the change. We go and come and serve. But evidently we are not seen. We do not seem to need food or sleep. I suppose we absorb moisture. I think our tenuous bodies are composed like clouds. But I do not know. Any way, your boy's heart is still in the right place.

Bob repeatedly stressed the need to get all of this information to other parents in order to comfort them and asked his mother not to back away from the book project because she is laughed at. He added that he did not think it wise to get messages for others. He further informed his mother that those on his side knew nothing about the outcome of the war or if there was some cosmic purpose to such war, though in the great scheme of things it might not be as terrible as people in the earth life view it.

We must start on the fact that the soul is immortal. There is no death for the individual. As so many – even material-minded men – realize, the body is an exchangeable garment and does not count in the history of the man. It seems that there has been an interminable number of races and nations lost in obscurity. They have moved on to other worlds, as this present race must be moved on. I do not know why civilization is allowed to reach a high mark before it is wiped off the slate. But there has been that rule, and so the Creator must have a purpose.

I asked one of the teachers, and he said that the earth is a prepatory planet. The human race is marked for an advanced existence and is brought to as high a degree of perfection as may be necessary to bring up the average. That is: The high degree of intelligence of the greater number lifts the lesser in the scale. We begin the new existence where we left off in the old. The more we have gained, the greater our advancement among far more favorable conditions. That is not clear. I'll get a better hold on the idea.

Boylan had heard the skeptical theory that automatic writing is nothing more than the writer's subconscious emanations, perhaps encouraged by wishful thinking – nothing more or less. She pondered on that.

Well maybe they are. I cannot say that they are not. For I do not know what subconsciousness is. What stuff it is made of. Whence it comes or whither it goes. Maybe it is the bridge, the link between the mortal and immortal part of man. Maybe it is the inherent life which all scientists from first to last, have sought without finding; that invisible stumbling block over which every well-built theory of atoms and electrons takes its headlong fall. If subconsciousness is one of these, it is more than probable that my boy is using its avenue of communication. For they must be clear enough from his end of the road...

Bob dwells upon the simplicity of it all...[However] he finds it difficult to describe what the difference is in what we call the spiritual world: the ways of living, eating, drinking, and dressing...

There are a number of dogs with us. I do not know whether they are astral dogs or not. They look just the same to me, and they go with us and help with our work. The boys who come out are simply delighted to see them.

Jack Wells is back with us and in immediate command of our company. He has been to see his mother and he is one happy boy. She is somewhere here. Has been out for a long time. But one of the messengers found him for her and he got immediate leave to go. That sounded pretty good to me, He will tell me about things later. We are very busy.

I have had up to the time that I began to arrange for publishing, almost daily communication from my son. Some of these are personal letters which I shall not include in this work, lest in the future some one may pierce our necessary anonymity. But these that seem to me to clear somewhat the mystery, and to simplify the methods of mental intercourse, are given as received.

The remainder of the book sets forth Bob's messages with no further commentary from his mother. Selected comments from Bob's messages (headings added) follow:

Credulity: It is a funny thing that people always want to accept the most difficult creeds and to believe the most elusive doctrines. They (people) are a bundle of credulity and stubborn doubt. Of course their eyes will be opened in good time. But think what peace of mind they are missing.

Spirit Influence: I told you that we are not given any power over bullets. That we can comfort but not save from what you call death. That is not quite the case, I find. Jack Wells directed me to stand by a junior lieutenant today and impel him this way or that to avoid danger. In this way I discovered that my perceptions are much more sensitive than they were before I came out. I can estimate the speed and determine the course of shells. I stood by this fellow and nudged him here and there, kept him from being hurt. I asked Wells if that was an answer to prayer. Wells said, "No, the young chap is an inventor, and has a job ahead of him that's of importance to the world." An older man spoke up and said, "Prayers are answered. Don't make any mistake about that. But they are not answered according to material ways of looking at things." I did not get his explanation well enough to venture to repeat it. I'll know more, probably as I go on.

Spirit Travel: I have not seen any one with wings. We cover any number of miles without fatigue. That is a good thing, for I have not heard of any rest from labor being advocated. We do however, rest others. We ease the boys in the trenches – they wonder how they can sleep as comfortably on the hard, wet ground, and for several nights, now, I have been holding a sick boy in my arms. Those duties keep us occupied almost all the time, but we have undiminished force and are never weary. I hear continually of the presence of the Savior on the battle fields. I think this must be true. Anyway, the dying are certain that He has been with them, and they are happy. They speak of His love.

Many Dimensions: Tell this to mothers. Jack Wells talked with me last night, and he gave me a great description of what he saw when he went away for his visit. His mother heard that he had gone west, and she sent a messenger for him. It seems that the messengers are somewhat different from the rest of us. I will speak of that later. Jack accompanied this messenger. They pierced the envelope of the earth. Or at least found some exit. From what Jack gleaned, he thought the world we have believed to be so tremendously powerful is really much like the smallest ball in the nest of balls that are carved out of ivory by Orientals. One within the other, you know. You have to penetrate one to gain access to another of larger size. So, as I understand it, the spiritual worlds of our solar system are swung into space, not separately, but together, each on its own axis but all moving in harmony as one. The progress of the soul is through these spheres up to the highest development. The earth is the material or lowest form. We have often wondered why Christ came to save our little planet when He seemed to belong equally to the whole Universe. But it seems that this is the cradle of humanity. That herein was established the race of men, an independent order of creation that was to acquire through knowledge of sin and pain and sacrifice, a strength that should fit men for leadership among supermen. Jack's mother is in the next world, and from what he says I was not right about the manner of living. His mother received him in a house where other members of the family were waiting for him, and it was just a happy reunion. While he was conscious that they had all passed through the experience of death, he could not really see any change in their appearances. They were dressed in what appeared to be fabrics but were probably vapor stuff, and they seemed to eat, drink, and live much as they lived on earth. It is said that business is conducted along ideal lines, and agriculture is brought to perfection. There are many chemists and inventors at work to develop resources, and as the different globes are intercommunicable, the earth gets the benefit of the discoveries. This figure is often used and I guess it is a good one. Consider the system of planets all incorporated in a final atmospheric envelope as so many rooms in a school. All doors are open for the entrance and exit of every one, high or low, in the whole school; the separations are mental. A pupil can jump over any grade if he has the ability. Those who qualify on earth can enter advanced classes or conditions.

Reincarnation: The return or reincarnation of a spirit is a matter concerning which I am not informed. I know that many return many times. I do not as yet understand how this is accomplished, or whether it is voluntary or an arbitrary law. I hope I shall not have to go back. I'd rather take a fling among the other worlds. I could not be your boy; and I'd rather have you than any other mother.

Soul Mates: Jack's mother and sister are teachers. It is the business of those who are familiar with the law of the place to instruct others. Ruth Wells was killed in an automobile accident a day or so before she was to have been married. Her lover went out with the Canadians and has been doing great work in the air. He came out (died) while Jack was there, and he came straight to Ruth with a messenger she had sent to wait for his arrival. Now they are incorporated in one form. I do not quite understand this yet. I shall have to see the married to know what that means. But I am told that a man and woman are really one. Each half of a whole. When they are mates they are united. The matter of plural marriages is settled in this way. The real mates are brought together. The others finding their complementary selves. It is a difficult subject. Better leave it out of the question until I get it in clearer shape. I do not know which side dominates this dual personality. I talked it over with a group of fellows here – those who have just come out – and some of us like the idea.

(A later message) I heard that the married become incorporated in one body. That is not just as it seemed at first to be. The two who love and marry are one in spirit and act and think as one soul. But they are separable in form and able to pursue their independent ways.

Grief: As I told you, some of us are assigned to escort duty. When the boys come west – quote that – we meet and guide them across the Invisible Line. Most of them feel perfectly fit when they come. But some few are confused or frightened. Particularly about the sorrow of those they leave behind. Try and make this point plain to the families. The boys are all right. Do not mourn for them. Every tear tortures the dead. Know that they are loving their folks and anticipating a meeting. I must go.

Family Ties: The most important thing for us to consider is this: We are just as much alive as we ever were, and the ties of love continue. This does not necessarily mean the ties of relationship. Love is the dominating force. For instance, the fact that I am your son, born of your body, is not the thing that will unite us in this advanced life. There is a subtler bond which has nothing to do with consanguinity. Spiritual affiliation or sympathy is about what that is, as well as I can make out.

But I am not yet far enough advanced to make any definite or authoritative statement I only want to start this whole propaganda of comfort, on the one sure thing: *There is no death.*

Evil: This is during a lull in battle. I inquired of the teacher why the German soldiers are so devoted to the Kaiser, how blind belief of millions came to be fixed on this one weak madman. For he is a lunatic. It was explained that a Mesmeric wave has swept Germania from the throne to the far borders since William's grandfather ruled. Mesmer, the Austrian, set forces into operation then, which he has maintained since through the mind of the present Kaiser.

I do not know whether that is a fact of science or a personal opinion. The man who told me is a stranger to me. He may not have any real information.

Fear of Death: Mother, I have found out another thing from this point of view. There is little or no fear of death among men who go into battle. The soul seems to remember, suddenly, that it may be about to repeat an interesting experience. The physical side of the soldier is dominated by the spiritual and carried on with a kind of thrilling joy. The meanest man sometimes surprises his comrades by exhibitions of courage. This is the reason. In this connection I must mention Cooper. You will remember that I wrote you about him when I enlisted. He seemed to be the one bloke on our regimental 'scutcheon. A sniveling "willy boy" who was afraid to go home in the dark. We all wondered how he stood the examiner's gaff and was accepted. He had prayed, very likely, that he would be turned down. Well, he came west since I last wrote you. I happened to be near when the grenade fell in the trench and saw him grab it in his arms and scramble out with it before it exploded. He saved a whole company, among them many wounded. I went with him over the top and yelled, "Bully for you, Coop, old man!" Then the bomb blew away his mortality, and he saw me. We left the field together, and I took him back among the hills where the particular group of helpers headed by Jack Wells gave him a glad hand. He's all right and a trump among us. Get word to his mother.

Christian Resistance: I got your word about the difficulties you are meeting in conveying the information (to Cooper's mother). Isn't it curious that the human mind instinctively rejects the easiest answer to a problem? Well get such comfort across as you can, but do not try to convince anyone that you communicate with me. You would probably be carted off to a padded cell if you should tell all we shall talk about. For I feel that we shall get on further soon. Wells says a new company is to relieve us, and we will "proceed to our destination."

Cooper is in a blue funk about his mother. She is frantic with grief, and he cannot communicate with her. She is like many Christians. She subscribes to a creed – but she doesn't believe it. If she would just take her pencil in her hand, and let Coop do the rest! Then she would come to know that her son and all the other sons are living and only kept from being happy and full of new and splendid ambitions by the tears of those they love on earth. To mourn is natural, but it really isn't natural to be hopeless.

Criticism: I got that little hint you wired me about knocking Christians. You see I still need your bully judgment. I remember your little old tenet that no cause is won by criticism. And I believe we have a cause, mother. Of course this matter of automatic writing, as you call it, is old and generally discredited. Some big, independent thinkers know that it is genuine in the main. But most folks are from Missouri. You have to show them something that can't be shown to material senses before they consent to be comforted. Too bad, isn't it?

Spiritual Bodies: As far as I can make out, we are going to a very real world: a globe divided into parts of land and water: one of the near stars, maybe. I'll find out about that. We are, I am informed, much the same as we were before we came; except that we are no longer limited or hampered by the flesh and bone body we formerly occupied. We have "raised spiritual bodies" just like the old Book says. But it is the spirit that quickeneth, isn't it? So there you are. We are still folks – and not still folks either – nobody dumb here, as far as I can learn.

Coloring the Messages: Mother, dear, when you are writing for me, be rather careful not to interpolate. You do not, much. But we want this to be pretty direct, don't we? Our only object now is to get this comfort – this possibility of communication between the seen and the unseen living – to those that mourn. You do not feel any fatigue or strain, do you? ...This is simply thought transference, dictation. A perfectly natural thing. Induce others to get into communication with these boys who want to butt in while I talk to you. I am besieged to give you addresses. But if you can get any publisher to take these notes, I guess that will be the best to get an audience. Try — or —. They are both good firms and liberal thinkers.

The Savior: Emphasize this, mother. For every boy that is hurt or terrified, there is a comforter. I write you that we hear, continually, that the Savior is often seen on the fields. I have not dared to look, sometimes, when I have felt, rather than seen, a strange soft light. I am not ready to look just now. But there is no doubt but that He moves among the soldiers. I am called away.

(A later message) I was easing a boy in my arms; but he was very young, and he wanted his mother. I could not comfort him. Some One beside me said: "I will take him." I could not look up. But I knew Who it was. Let mothers hear of this.

Beyond Language: I get all your messages, mother. I can only answer a few questions. Partly because I am not yet sure of many things here and partly because there seems to be no means of communication concerning certain conditions. That is: when we get beyond the usual, we are beyond the common medium of language. The words we know are inadequate to express our revelations. Of course until we move on into the Big Places, we are really on almost the same footing as though I too were in the flesh. But when the Big Places are reached, I shall have more difficulty in conveying my information. At least, so I suppose. Now I am to continue in the ether for a time anyway. Ought to pick up considerable news for you. If I dwell on things that seem the least important, perhaps it is because of this single of vision. Now the all important matter to the boys here is to have their folks know that they are alive and well and filled with intense enthusiasm and ambition. Take up the Bible and read it with this that I am telling you in mind. I expect, as time goes on, I shall be able to describe scenes and customs to you – after the manner of the observant teachers – but now what you must learn is this: In this intermediate place which is neither wholly material nor wholly spiritual, we are busy and so happy, or would be if it were not for the sobs and tears of our folks. Please do not give way to sadness, mother. And for heaven's sake (this is laterally for heaven's sake) beg the mourners to stop crying, and to cease wearing black clothes.

Meeting Deceased Relatives: I have not met any relatives. You know we are still on earth. Some of the boys who have folks in far places get leave to go and see them. But I feel that my job is right here. A while ago I lifted up a wounded color-bearer, and together we kept the flag from touching the ground. That seemed to be his main idea. I held him until relief came and promised to wait in case he should come west. But he is to recover.

Suicide: Warn all with whom you talk against suicide. I do not gather from what I hear that curses afflict any poor soul that makes that mistake. But the self-inflicted death disarranges and delays the plans that are being shaped for the individual. Every detail of life is worked out with a thoroughness only possible in spiritual geometry. A sudden break necessitates rebuilding the whole theory. It may require skill for you to tell what you have to tell and yet restrain broken-hearted ones from throwing themselves across the invisible line. Of course, they want to rejoin their darlings. But that will be later.

Convincing Skeptics: Think of the situation this way: A child, for instance, is screaming and sobbing in the terrors of nightmare. The mother tries to waken him, to reassure him, and tell him that he is safe in her arms, against her breast, that all is right. But she cannot make him listen and understand. There you have it. It's the same thing, exactly... Don't argue. We cannot convince anyone against his will. Let him believe, or deny. You are only a messenger. One accepts the heartease you offer, or he does not.

Moving to Higher Realms: We do not know when we are to be sent on to some other field. You remember we were once recalled when we had almost reached an important port of departure from this environment. The subject of these points of egress interests me greatly. It seems that there are certain defined avenues of intercommunication. We do not fly up and into some other sphere. We travel by established channels. I am very anxious to find out just what this means, and I shall hope to let you know. There must be some reason why, of all the millions who have passed the lines, no one has defined the boundaries of the unseen world. We talk the matter over, here, and have about agreed that language becomes inadequate or we write upon untranslatable conditions. Then, too, we may begin to count time by the thousand-year schedule. With the realization that you will soon be with us, we do not think to send you descriptions of what you are to see. One thing we must not lose sight of. This is the land of the living, and the loved ones are safe.

Dual World: Mother, it is not a new thought, but it is true that all forms of life are created dual. We have spoken of the human and spiritual only briefly because I am crassly ignorant, even yet. But Nature is also two-sided; material and ethereal. Everything is duplicated, forest, stream, landscape. Does that fact not make my place of residence more tangible to you? I should have told you sooner if I had heard of it.

Near-Death Experience: I have permission to tell you that Cooper has, because of his understanding and compassion, been sent back home as an instructor. His body, sustained by some life principle which I cannot explain, has been all this time in a reconstruction hospital back of the French lines. You may see him with your own eyes. And you will know that any man who has crossed No Man's Land, and returned, has a message to the world from God.

(A later message) Cooper will take up his old life on earth, and his mother will have her son. But he will not be the same. None of those who go back will be the same. Angels, dressed in stained and faded khaki, will walk the familiar streets. Listen to them.

Communication Difficulties: As I have said before, I shall, perhaps, enter into less translatable conditions. The common speech may be inadequate. That, alone, may account for the futile messages transmitted through mediums. Still the spirit is free to travel, and it is likely I may find a way to continue my letters to you and to give you such information as may be permitted.

Animals: Dogs come and go freely, back and forth across the invisible line. I am told this as a fact. They do not need to leave their natural bodies to associate with those who have died. They often follow their masters. Other animals have not quite these privileges, but after dissolution they appear here. I may not be clear. I often find a certain embarrassment in saying things that I, myself, would once have called bunk. But I guess they are true, all right.

Appearance: We look as we did in the flesh. It seems almost as though we had only slipped out of our skins, as the snakes do. A natural process, familiar to simple people, but too simple to be considered by those butterfly hunters that try to net the soul.

Christ: Christ walks among the wounded continually. The dying see Him, and the hurt are healed by His hand. Many have told me, and several times I have felt Him near. Once, for a moment, I saw Him. I told you.

Spiritual Vision: We are passing through a land laid waste and yet triumphant. I felt immensely surprised to see in all its beauty one great cathedral that had been destroyed. The angel said that all such buildings of prayer and song are spiritual and beyond vandal desecration. The bricks will be restored to conform to the imperishable idea. I do not want to get metaphysical (in the bewildering way). I just want to say that I am improving in spiritual vision. When we started out before, you remember, I was only able to see the obvious; broke bodies of flesh and of stone. Today I see the immortal structures.

The Simple Truth: Life is continuous and souls go marching on. That's the big truth. All other things can be added unto it. Many things I say are not authoritative. But this thing is. Look in the Bible, with these spectacles on, and see. As far as modes of living, habits of angels, philosophies and opinions, my reports are likely to be as accurate as the average traveler in an unfamiliar country.

CHAPTER THREE

CLAUDE

Background: *Second Lieutenant Claude Herschel Kelway-Bamber. a pilot attached to the Royal Flying Corps, was killed in action on November 15, 1915, when his plane was shot down while fighting two German planes near Courtral, Flanders. He was 20 years and six months old at the time.*

Claude had joined the Army immediately after the outbreak of the war in August 1914 and was commissioned as an officer two months later, then sent to pilot training. He was the son of Herbert and Eliza Kelway-Bamber of Hyde Park Mansions, London. His father was employed as an engineer for Leeds Forge Co. Claude was interred at Harlebeke New British Cemetery in Belgium.

Claude's story is set forth in "Claude's Book" first published in 1918 by Methuen & Co., with a sequel, "Claude's Book II," published in 1920. The "editor" of the two books is shown as L. Kelway-Bamber, his mother, who may have preferred the name Liza to Eliza.

Outside of the Introduction, the book is a collection of spirit messages from Claude, written in the first person, with no commentary by his mother. Hence, she considered herself the editor rather than the author. While the messages came through the mediumship of Gladys Osborne Leonard, the same medium featured in the first chapter of this book and discussed in the Introduction, the presentation of the messages is somewhat different than in Chapter One. Although the messages from Claude were relayed by "Feda," Mrs. Leonard's spirit control, Mrs. Kelway-Bamber presents them as if coming directly from Claude, avoiding the "he says," and confusion apparent in the more strictly verbatim recording by Sir Oliver Lodge in Chapter One. Like Sir Oliver, she corrects Feda's grammatical gaffes (Sir Oliver left a few grammatical errors in his transcripts for effect, but Mrs. Kelway-Bamber corrects them all.)

In the Introduction to the second book, Dr. Ellis T. Powell, a renowned British barrister and journalist, states that he believes that Claude was being used as an intermediary by higher spiritual sources, and that he (Claude) was "not fully alive to the full purport of that which he was transmitting." Such a theory is consistent with other teachings suggesting that advanced spirits find it more difficult to communicate with those on the earth plane than lower spirits because of the difference in vibration; therefore, they employ the spirits at a lower vibration to relay the information on to those in the earth vibration.

In the Introduction, Mrs. Kelway-Bamber writes that on February 29, 1916, she attended a public séance in which Mrs. Brittain was the clairvoyant. She did not know Mrs. Brittain or any one else in the room. She makes no mention of any evidential readings while there. However, while on her way home and waiting for a train in the underground, she found herself standing next to Mrs. Brittain. She made some remark to Mrs. Brittain about the meeting and was surprised when Mrs. Brittain told her that a "spirit boy" was with her. She described the young man as tall, slight, and fair, blue eyes, smooth hair, well brushed on his forehead, which was well developed. She added that he was boyish-looking, with smooth, clear skin, and a very happy, merry disposition. This description matched Claude exactly.

Two weeks later, on March 14, Mrs. Kelway-Bamber had a sitting with Mrs. Leonard. As was customary, she did not give her name or any clue as to whom she was hoping to hear from. After Mrs. Leonard entered the trance state, Feda immediately identified Claude and said he was wearing a grey suit. This was quite a surprise to Mrs. Kelway-Bamber as she had been looking for the suit the day before to give it to a young man she knew.

Claude told her that he was wearing the suit to prove to her that he was with her when she was searching for it. Feda then said that he was showing her a medal, which confused her, as she assumed he would have shown himself in an Army uniform if he had been a soldier. She could tell that he had not died of an illness, then received a "rushing feeling" as if he were falling. As Mrs. Kelway-Bamber did not want to dwell on how he died, she asked Feda to go beyond that. Feda told her that Claude had been with her recently when she climbed a stile into some woods, which was definitely evidential as she had just returned *from such a trek in Scotland. Claude asked her if she had received some photos of him and his soldier friends "ragging" outside a tent. She had not, but such photos were received later.*

On April 10, Mrs. Kelway-Bamber attended another public séance, the medium being a Mr. Von Bour, an absolute stranger to her. He came to her and described some spirit friends he could see with her before giving a very accurate description of Claude. He also mentioned a "George," whom she recognized, and a "John," whom she did not recognize. At a sitting with Mrs. Leonard sometime later, Claude informed his mother that "John" was her brother, who had died at the age of four and had grown up in spirit. Even then, she did not appreciate the "John" message, because he would have been about 40, not 20, as Von Bour stated. Claude explained that spirits reach a prime age in the spirit life and do not age.

At another sitting with Mrs. Leonard on November 11, Claude told his mother that his spirit body was just the same as his physical body had been, "down to the wart on my finger." This was very evidential as Mrs. Kelway-Bamber recalled suggesting to Claude that he see the doctor and have the wart removed. At another sitting with Mrs. Leonard, Claude brought a spirit friend who had passed over only a few days before, but his death was not announced until a week later.

There was more in the way of evidence for Mrs. Kelway-Bamber, but the book is not about evidence. It is about Claude's experiences on the Other Side.

Reader alert: *All paragraphs below in standard print are communication from Claude, (as relayed through Feda), often abridged, while those in italics are those of the editor of this book.*

✳✳✳

I was rather depressed as I went out to my machine that last November morning. I don't know why. I certainly had no presentiment of evil; but, once started, my spirits rose as usual, and I felt quite cheery and singularly free from nervousness.

Many men here have since told me this rather curious fact, that on the occasion of their last fight, whether in the air or in the trenches, nervousness left them. I don't know whether the spirit instinctively knows its fate and braces itself to meet it, or if one's spirit friends are able to make their presence and comfort felt at that supreme crisis, but probably it was the only occasion on which I was absolutely free of all fear.

When we were attacked by two enemy aeroplanes my feeling was one of acute irritation for we were on our way back after finishing some work over the enemy lines. I felt harassed, too, as I climbed and turned and dived here and there to attack. My observer said something and I remember getting the nose of the machine down to get below one of our opponents, when I felt a terrible blow on my head, a sensation of dizziness and falling, and then nothing more.

It may have been a fortnight or more later – we have no account of "time" here, so I can not be sure – that I became conscious again. I felt dizzy and stupid but was not in pain, and on collecting my thoughts and looking round found myself in bed in an unknown room.

Before thought took definite form I felt I had been passing through space. My body seemed to have become light. I wondered if I was in hospital, and if anyone had written to tell you I was wounded. Nurses moved about the room; if I attempted to talk or ask questions a doctor came to my side, and putting his hand on my head soothed me to silence again.

Several more days must have passed. I rested, dozing and peaceful; it never seemed to get dark.

On one occasion when the kindly doctor came to my bedside I asked him where I was, and if my people knew of my whereabouts. He did not soothe me to sleep, as usual, but sat down beside me.

"I want to have a talk with you and explain things," he said "You are not on the earth now; you are no longer on the physical plane."

I didn't understand, and asked, "Surely I am in a private hospital?"

"No," he replied; you have passed out of the physical body and are in the state you used to know as having died."

I could not believe him. "Great Scot! You don't mean I'm dead!"

"We will use that term simply as it's the only one you understand just now,' he said. "You are alive and are starting the fuller and more beautiful life"; but the feeling I had was one of sudden loss and loneliness and almost desperation.

"Is my mother here, or have my father or brother come? If they are not here I don't want to stay!"

Claude continued to struggle in his "awakening," saying that he felt as if he were in a dream. Still thinking he was in some kind of hospital, he told a guide that he wanted to see his mother and became very indignant with the guide, who advised him to be more patient. Then a man came to

him and identified himself as Claude's grandfather, but since Claude had
never met his grandfather when alive in the flesh, he was not convinced.

Others came who claimed to be relatives and friends, including several ladies who kissed me, but as I knew none of them I remained inconsolable, and my friend, the doctor, promised as soon as it was suitable I should be sent to see you, that the truth might be proved to me. A few days later I was told I was to be taken home to see you.

I can't remember the exact details of that evening, as I was shaken with conflicting emotions which chased through me – joy, and fear, and hope, and grief, and impatience, and almost despair of the unknown future into which I had plunged without you.

I passed with the two friends who guided me through the astral plane to the earth. As we came nearer, the atmosphere became thicker and misty, and the houses and everything seemed indistinct, the view disappeared, and I found myself standing in your room at the foot of your bed. A terrible feeling of despair filled my heart, for I knew what I had been told was true. I was indeed "dead."

You were sitting up in bed in an agony of grief, the tears streaming down your face, repeating my name over and over again, and calling me, and saw me not. I had expected a cry of joy, but it never came. I bent forward and called as loudly as I could, "Mummy, I'm here; can't you see or hear me?"

You made no reply. I went to your side and put my arms round you, and though you were not conscious of my presence I seemed to be able to soothe you, for you became calmer and lay down.

I felt as if I were fainting and had no will to resist when my guides took me away back to the hospital. I felt, however, that your love was mine still. I could feel its power. I understood it and realized it better than ever before. It was a spiritual caress, and I felt it through every fibre of my body, and was full of thankfulness. I knew, too, that in all my life your love had never failed me, and that even now, you would find a way, if it were possible, to bridge the gulf between us – you would never let me "drop out." When I realized this, I knew the worst was over, and the bitterness of death had passed. Worn by my emotions, I slept and woke later in quite a different mood.

I found a young man seated at my bedside, who said, "Well, old chap, we've pulled through." He has since become a friend of mine; his name is "Joe." You did not know him personally, but you know of him and know whom I mean.

A sense of adventure now filled my mind: I felt full of health and well-being, and was longing to explore this new country.

Claude was then accompanied by Joe, his grandfather, and a number of other relatives and friends to a home that was made ready for him. It consisted of a bedroom, a den with a piano as well as a delightful garden and accommodations for other men.

I asked one of my guides if it was a "thought-world" we were in, though the ground felt quite substantial to my feet; and he said, "It is more real and permanent than the one you have left." I bent down and poked my finger in the soil and found it left a hole, and the soil stuck under my nail.

Upon seeing a beautiful fountain, Claude cupped his hands and drank a little. He asked his guide what would happen if he drank too much and was told that it would be foolish. The guide added:

> "If you were foolish you would not be here, as each man earns his environment by his conduct. By the working of the natural law you gravitate to the place for which you are suited; what is within you draws you automatically."

> I bathed in a glorious lake the water of which was slightly scented. It ran off my body as I stepped out, almost as if it were running off marble or alabaster.

> I became accustomed to my new life and found innumerable friends, both new and old; all were ready and anxious to help me in every way.

Claude told his mother that he did not think of death very often, even though he faced it every day in combat, because it seemed so indefinite. He considered the possibility that he would be killed and hoped he would find himself in heaven, but heaven did not sound very appealing to him as he did not think of it as anything more than sitting on a throne on a cloud in a white robe, while playing a harp. It sounded terribly boring to him.

I know now the whole mistake lies in looking upon death as the end of "activity," with a renewal at some indefinite date, whereas as a matter of fact it is an incident only, though a very important one, in a continuous life. Your feelings, your memory, your love, your interests and ambitions remain; all you have left behind, and even that which one cannot at first realize, is the physical body, which proves to be merely the covering of the spiritual to enable it to function in a material world. Man truly is a spirit and has a body, not vice versa.

I have told you that I, in common with hundreds of other men here, go down to the battlefields to help to bring away the souls of those who are passing out of their bodies. We are united for the work, having ourselves endured the horrors of war. Spirits unused to it cannot bear the terrible sights and sounds. We bring them away so that they may return to consciousness far from their mutilated physical bodies, and oh, Mum, I feel quite tired sometimes of explaining to men that they are "dead"!

They wake up feeling so much the same; some go about for days, and even months, believing they are dreaming.

Death works no miracle, and you wake up here the same personality exactly that left the earth-plane. Your individuality is intact, and your "spirit body" a replica of the one you have left, down to small details – even deformities remain, though, I am told they lessen and disappear in time.

People with narrow, set, and orthodox beliefs are puzzled by the reality, the "ordinaryliness," if I may coin a word, of the spirit world. If it were described to them as "flashes of light," "mauve and sapphire clouds," "golden rivers," etc., it would more readily approximate with their preconceived ideas. They require "mystery" about the future life. I often laugh when I hear them complain they can't believe in "solid" things like houses, and gardens in the spirit-world...

The first time I was sent down to help our enemies I objected but was told to remember they were fighting for what they believed to be right and in defence of their country, too. I saw rather an interesting meeting between an Englishman and a German who had killed each other. They met face to face and looked at each other steadily. The Englishman held out his hand. His erstwhile enemy, taking it, said, "What d— fools we have been!"

As a matter of fact, I am not doing so much battlefield work as many of the others, and only go when there has been severe fighting and there is a great deal to do. Sometimes we are needed. I am being trained to be a teacher. Yes, darling, I know you are surprised; but, you remember I used to be good at explaining things; besides, you know too I was rather "bossy."

Claude said that he had been studying science – the science of life, the cause of things, and natural law – and that he had learned there is no such thing as a "miracle" or "supernatural," although it might be "supernormal." Man can create nothing, he was taught, but rather all new discoveries are further knowledge of how to use latent force or power.

I realize enough even in this short time, to know that the more one learns the more truly humble one becomes, because it is only then possible to know of the vast untouched fields of knowledge yet to be explored, and it is only very ignorant people in these days who say anything is 'impossible," because it happens to be beyond their particular understanding.

As to the theory that spiritual truths would have been "revealed" to us if we have been intended to know them, that is an argument that might be equally well applied to material matters. Neither railways, telegraphs, telephones, microscopes. X-rays, nor any other modern invention has been "revealed" to mankind without hard work; and if these "temporal things" have required so much effort, why should anyone imagine that the spiritual things, which, being eternal, are so infinitely more valuable should be given to man without any trouble on his part?

After all, spiritual things can only be spiritually discerned. It is only striving for truth that makes the spirit grow; to lull it into a state of lethargy does not help it develop.

I tell you what it is: unless the Church wakes up and moves with the times it will cease to exist in the future. The war has given it a great opportunity. Men will no longer be content with platitudes and unreasoning belief. You must satisfy their minds as well as their hearts, which is possible now that science and religion are not antagonistic.

Men cannot now be frightened with tales of hell fire. They have learned that many roads lead to God. There is no "right of way" which is a perquisite of any particular form of religion. The only one that will influence men at all is one that is full of common sense, that makes everyday life worth living, and death no longer a dreaded visitor but even a friend, for indeed it may be that.

This knowledge would not make earth life of less but of greater value, for we should then realize and appreciate the fact that we are in the world to be trained, to develop character and learn self-discipline. It would teach us to bear trials bravely and with understanding that now seem uncalled for and senseless. We should know that this earth life is only the "school time" and preparation of the fuller life that follows...

I don't understand the people who say that "spirit return is possible, but wrong," because only "devils" or "evil spirits" can communicate. Surely God would not reserve this, His great comfort and gift, the assurance of continued conscious existence, solely for the wicked?

Claude said he was living on the third sphere or plane, what some people call "Summerland" and others call "Paradise." He said that "eating" for him involves absorbing all the nourishment his body requires from the atmosphere. Although he doesn't actually sleep, he does feel tired at times and rests, refreshing himself by bathing in the lake.

Nothing can kill the soul, not even man himself; though sometimes, if before the final separation of body and soul the illness has been very severe, there has been brain disease, or the end has been violent and sudden, the shock to the soul is very great, and it may remain in a state of unconsciousness for many days or weeks, till it is recovered sufficiently to awake in its new conditions. You see, therefore, a suicide far from escaping trouble only goes from one form of misery to another; he cannot annihilate himself and pass to nothingness.

How do I get about? I walk very often, at other times if necessary I generate sufficient power, which I concentrate by effort of will within my body, to take me anywhere with the speed of thought. Our bodies are so light and so strong, it is easy to jump the highest wall with the slightest effort; the atmosphere has not the same resisting power to our bodies as it has to yours...

When I first came over, I longed for you to be here but I was told that your earth work was not accomplished, and I must be patient – there are so many wonderful things I want to show you and to tell you about.

One reason why we have found it so easy to get in touch with each other is because we are both psychic. Of course we, neither of us, realized it before, but I can quite clearly understand and see it now, and I see other things so differently too in the light of all the knowledge I have gained. Music, and flowers, and things I should have thought it rather "sentimental" to admire before, I thoroughly appreciate now. In the spirit world there is a stronger affinity between the spirit and beautiful things than between any physical connection on the earth plane, perhaps because it is a more perfect expression of God.

Concerning work, Claude went on to say that each man does that for which he is best fitted, and that all work is done under beautiful conditions. And while certain forms of labor are looked down upon on earth, all work there is recognized as valuable. He said that many things are made there, just as they are on the earth plane, but there they rely largely on "gases." Beginning at the lowest sphere, these gases rise to suitable environments – a law of the universe which he did not understand. These gases are sometimes concentrated into solids by chemical action, and from them are made bricks for houses, material for clothes, etc.

You want to know about clothes? Well, you can wear just what you like here; there are no fashions to follow or appearances to keep up. Though a very mixed array is the consequence it does not seem incongruous, for here you dress to express yourself and not to impress your neighbors.

I dress as I did with you, but some people wear white robes because they think when out of the mortal body it is the correct thing to do. If I chose to wear a tunic and sandals, or a "Beefeater's" get up, no one would laugh and jeer; they would realize it made me happy, and that is reason enough.

Mummy, dear, I quite understand how difficult all I tell you about my life here is for you to realize. I am quite sure in your place I should never believe it, but it's true all the same!

The more one studies science the more possible it seems to become. After all, the difficulty is in believing in things so real, so strong, so substantial, and yet to most people invisible. Yet, when you come to think of it, on earth, there are many of the most "solid" things made of gases and elements which in their pure state are invisible. A large proportion of our physical bodies, rocks, and some of the earth itself, for instance, are made of oxygen, which is impalpable as well as invisible.

Undeveloped people are those who live only through the senses and have not cultivated the intellect nor the spirit. To them what is impalpable seems "impossible."

Claude proceeded to tell his mother that he had gone down to the astral plane, searched for, and made friends with a murderer, a man who had been executed for killing his wife. Finding him was not a matter of curiosity but an assignment of sorts in which he had to trace the cause leading to the tragedy and find the "kink" in the man's character which made the deed seem excusable to him.

He found "X" to be a very "decent chap," fond of animals and children, a quiet inoffensive little fellow. He claimed that he was driven mad by his wife, an "odious" woman who drank to excess, constantly nagged him, and was unfaithful. He reached a point where he just couldn't take it any more and became desperate.

Following his transition, he struggled for about a year in earth time, full of hate and rage, before he began to calm down and realize he had no right to take her life. As soon as this realization came, friends from higher realms began to help him. He was now working with others who came over with misery and bitterness as he had, thereby improving his condition.

Claude's mother expressed concern that she was delaying his progress by keeping in touch with her. Claude responded:

You do not delay my progress, as was suggested to you, by keeping in touch with me. People on earth will not realize that you cannot "summon" spirits any more than you can compel men on earth to come and see you if they do not wish to do so. In the spirit world, people choose what is best for their own evolution.

If mortals desire the companionship of spirit friends merely for purposes of material gain, it does not of course do either of them much good; but when love is the motive and mutual help the desire, it is good for both, for helping others in the way of progress.

There is a wedge now being driven in to open the door between the two worlds of matter and spirit, and I love to feel that I may be a tiny splinter of that wedge.

This is an excellent opportunity of letting a little light and hope through which will help mankind, for I have explained to you the creative power of thought. At present the earth is enveloped in what looks like a thick grey mist caused by the thoughts of cruelty, rage, grief, and pain that are continually outpouring.

On the first anniversary of Claude's transition to the spirit world, he told his mother that he sometimes feels as if it has been hundreds of years since he passed over. He said he feels that he has learned so much, but at the same time, he feels as if he is a little boy again, sitting at his mother's feet. His mother asked him if he had seen Christ.

Yes, I have seen Christ once, Mummy, and remembering how awe-inspiring the occasion was, cannot help wondering how anyone could imagine at death they could go straight to His kingdom, when most of us have done so little to earn that beatitude!

I was told I should be allowed to see Him, but honestly at the time I did not realize or appreciate the fact. I thought it would probably mean going to a very high church with an elaborate ritual of pomp and ceremony. When the appointed time came, my guides provided me with a plain white robe to wear, and we passed through connecting shafts to the Christ sphere.

My general impression was that of brightness, almost dazzling; the air scintillated like diamonds – it almost crackled, it was so full of electricity; my feet had not a very firm grip on the ground.

There were bands and processions of people, white-robed, all going in one direction. they moved with uplifted faces, singing beautiful music. We joined the rear of one group, and were almost swept along on a tide of intense feeling. We came to a building without any walls. It consisted of a roof, which seemed to be composed of interwoven rays of light of different colours, supported by pillars which looked as if they were made of mother-of-pearl.

There was a crowd of people all round, and raised above all others stood one glowing, radiant figure. I knew at once it was Christ, and instinctively fell on my knees, though He is not like any picture I have ever seen. I was so conscious of Him that I felt as if He was bending over me. His eyes seemed to penetrate me, and produce a wonderful glow. I felt uplifted in a culminating thrill of ecstasy. He was speaking, but I could not hear the words.

As I knelt there, many events of my life passed in review through my mind. I could visualize them as pictures. My memory seemed stored with records, not alone of the life I had just left, but of others in the far-away past; and as the various scenes presented themselves I seemed to realize the different lessons I had learned through these experiences and to know that all the events of my life had been leading up to this.

Concerning reincarnation, Claude informed his mother that they had been through many lives together, in different relationships, in different sexes, and in different connections, and that is why there is such an affinity between the two of them. He quipped that his mother was not Cleopatra, Helen of Troy, Boadicea, or any other famous person in history, to his knowledge.

I am told by friends here, that souls are sometimes reborn, reincarnated, in order to gain further experience, learn more life-lessons, or work out past sins and failings. Each earth life leaves its mark on character, and its lessons are forever imprinted on the subconscious mind, which registers everything that has ever happened to the soul from the beginning. This they say, explains much of the pain and trouble you see on earth. The sufferers are learning lessons which are necessary for their souls growth, for man was put into the world to develop the spiritual. They may have lived before, and neglected to learn them, or they may be new souls going through these experiences in one or other of the stages of their existence; it is all on the road of their evolution.

Families, friends, sections of nations in the revolving cycle of time reincarnated together very often, as they require the same experiences. When you begin to think seriously about the subject and look and study the people about you, you will be able to recognize that some people are old souls and others new.

Past experiences, though not consciously remembered, tone down crudities of character. Old souls have a sympathy, a strength, taught of pain and discipline, and are therefore considerate for others. When one knows many of the exceptionally gifted young men who have passed over in this war, one realizes they may have been old souls who gained their experience in the past and returned to earth for a glorious culmination in this supreme sacrifice.

I have often heard people ask why God permits wickedness. If it were impossible for man to sin, he would no longer be a free agent but an automation. As man is on earth to learn his lesson and develop his soul, he must have his mettle proved. There would be no good without evil. Contrasts exist and are necessary; just as day and night, wet and fine, heat and cold, pleasure and pain, are only realized and appreciated through their opposites.

Old souls have learnt also to keep in touch with and draw from the "God-force," the actual Source of Life. Psychically developed people are especially in contact with it.

The soul has a separate consciousness. Many people's souls leave their bodies in sleep habitually, or under anaesthetics, and travel to various places; some, on awaking are able to remember the scenes they have visited – and this memory can be cultivated. So you see the difference between sleep and death for some people is not very great after all, nor the passing painful nor difficult. It only means on one occasion they leave their bodies, to return no more.

Claude's guides showed him a number of pictures depicting his past lives with his mother. In the earliest one they were brother and sister in Egypt, both attached to the court of the Pharaoh. In a later life, in Palestine, they were both female, good friends, and early Christians. In a third scene, he saw them as brothers and members of a band of fighters.

I have never met a spirit yet who has seen God, and yet here you know you live because you are just a particle from the Divine.

You say it hurt you to hear the poor woman who spoke through the other medium the other day; she seemed so terribly unhappy and uncomfortable. Well, poor woman, she was so unready to pass out of the world. She was killed suddenly through an accident while in perfect health. She was a very worldly woman and could not believe it when she came to herself and found she had left her mortal body. She had no real belief in "life after death," and felt she was in a dream and a very unhappy one, for alas, for herself, she had in her life on earth laughed her husband out of all belief in it too! And she realized the difficulty she would have in undoing the mistake.

As you make the conditions of your own life after death by your state of spiritual development, you can imagine some people whose spiritual faculties have dwindled till they have become atrophied – almost a negligible quantity, in fact, can see no beauty here; in fact, they live under unpleasant conditions.

Some people are earthbound. All their interests are there, and they return for that contact with men and the old conditions they crave. I know it is difficult to understand why discarnate souls should still hanker after material and sometimes gross pleasures. It is because while in earth their senses ruled them, and stamped and coarsened the soul, instead of the spirit refining and purifying the body.

As I have already told you, for some time after people come here they continue to feel as if they were still in a mortal body. You can realize this in a small way from what is, alas, a common occurrence nowadays. Any soldier who has had the misfortune to lose a limb will tell you he can feel pain, discomfort, or irritation in it for days after it has been amputated.

In this way, spirits continue for some time after they have left them to "feel" their bodies after death, and you know from experience now that the first time a spirit returns through a medium the death condition is generally reproduced or indicated.

When his mother asked who appoints spirit guides or "guardian angels," Claude explained that no one appoints them, that they are spirit friends attracted by something in the individual which appeals to them and they try to influence and help those in whom they take an interest. Sometimes they are earth friends or relatives who have passed on and still have a bond of affection with the person, but other times they are strangers attracted by mutual interests, who try to inspire those still in the flesh. The interest might be religious, musical, scientific, art, medicine, or any other subject.

These things are being done every day, and the "flashes of genius" which illumine the world occasionally are the result of the influence of the spirit minds on the minds of those still in the world. When men realize it is possible to get help from these sources, they will do great things for those who have passed on; the sources of information, though not limitless, are vast in comparison with those on earth. The secrets of Atlantis and ancient Egypt are obtainable if they care to work to learn them.

I have told you, too, 'like attracts like." If a human being is spiritually and intellectually undeveloped, and lives only in the senses, the spirit friends he attracts are of a very undesirable order. They are the souls of those who had no wish to live anything but a life of animal gratification, and still hang about the world and their old haunts continually, trying to get a kind of second-hand indirect pleasure from the doings of the people who now follow in their footsteps.

Claude went on to tell his mother about some "charming Elementals." He explained that everything in animal life and the plant kingdom, in its highest development, takes on a certain resemblance to humanity. There are nature thought-forms, he said, some of which are made by the emanations, the "excess life," as it were, from flowers. These are the so-called "fairies" which are not just a figment of the imagination. They can be seen by people who live in touch with nature and who have unspoiled eyes. They have intelligences without being intellectual and are almost human in form.

I know you sometimes find it very difficult to follow my explanations, and I find it difficult to explain, for our experiences are limited, and language is limited and is inadequate to express spiritual things. It is like trying to explain the glories of a splendid sunset to a man who was born blind. After all, we can only judge things by past impressions, and when these are lacking we can only believe, if we are willing to accept them, through "faith, the evidence of things unseen."

You want to know what I feel about religion now, and if my ideas on reincarnation have changed my ideas of Christ. Well, darling, I will answer the last question first.

I believe that Christ is a great and wonderful personality, a great Spirit in the form of a man, as near as possible to God, because the God-force plays so strongly in and through Him, a fit instrument and receiver of that power.

There was a specific reason why Christ was sent. God specially directed Him; the consciousness of God within Him was very acute He knew He was the instrument and child of God. He was sent to be man's example for all time, to teach how pure, and holy, and simple and dignified, and useful, and beautiful life could be without any of the material aids of money or social position, and to prove the individual continuity of life after death. But He did not come to save men from the results of their sins. It is a comfortable theory but not true.

Here we learn that every man has to earn his own salvation. Sin is a breaking of God's laws, and carries its own inviolable consequences, which must be worked out by each individual personally. You might as well set the law of gravity in motion and expect it not to act...

As man evolves he gets nearer spiritual truth, and we know here that this is infinitely greater and more wonderful than anything ever yet told. One realizes the presentation of God usually taught on earth is utterly incorrect. He is not a glorified mortal sitting on a golden throne, not a vengeful nor jealous God – not, in a way, even a "personal" God to be propitiated to grant special gifts to a favoured few. He is not finite, but infinite: but because it is so difficult to realize so vast a fact, we feel on earth we want to locate and limit our idea of God to bring it within our understanding...

All life as projected into humans is therefore a "bit of God," and we are in consequence truly His sons and by that fact immortal.

When his mother asked Claude to give her details of a typical day in his life, Claude first explained that there is no time there, that time is a limitation only on the earth plane, so he could only attempt to explain it as a day in her time, beginning at midnight.

You know, for I have often told you, how when your body sleeps your soul comes over here and we spend hours together; you have sometimes dimly remembered things that happened as in a dream. Thousands of people come over in this way every night, and are more awake and alive while here than on earth in their mortal bodies. To do this, people must be spiritually evolved to a certain degree. Well, we go together to various places; sometimes we work on the third sphere among those who have just wakened in the spirit world, and are bewildered, and puzzled, and strange in their new surroundings. We explain to them where they are and bring their families to them.

I know it seems curious to you that you should be able to do this even better than I, as you are still in a mortal body; but that is the very reason. You see, you are the "half-way house," as it were, for along that little cord that connects your soul and body are travelling thoughts and desires of the world in which you live. You are therefore more in touch with the earth and bring its atmosphere with you, and so feel more familiar to one who has just come over. You are still controlled and limited by your earth-body, while connected with it.

Claude told his mother that the night before they had helped a boy who could not accept his new condition, when his mother, who had passed over two years earlier, came along. However, the boy's first comments were that he was now certain he had been dreaming since he knew his mother was "dead." They left the boy and his mother together, hoping that the mother would be able to convince him that he was no longer in the earth life. On another occasion, Claude took his mother on a tour of the higher spheres.

When it is time for you to return I take you back and then go home for a rest. I bathe in the lake, and, refreshed, go either to earth again to help on the battlefield, or if I am not required for that, I go on with my study of psychic laws.

After this, it would now be your afternoon. I have some recreation and amuse myself; later I go to look up friends on earth. On other days I listen to music, which is beautiful here beyond description; it thrills one. You know I used not to care very much about it on earth before I came over. Tell Daddy when he plays the piano in the evenings I see his music in "colours," all the same...

Occasionally I talk to most interesting people, men who were noted on earth and left their mark there as great statesmen, scholars, poets, musicians, teachers, etc. There, of course, I should never have known them – differences of age, wealth, position, etc., would have made it impossible. But here there are no artificial barriers, and a community of interest is a sufficient bond of friendship.

When Claude's mother expressed surprise that some of the people he had mentioned had not progressed higher, Claude informed her that they could have had they so desired, but many prefer to remain back to help out on the earth plane.

When you get beyond the third sphere, contact becomes more difficult, and it is only when you begin to feel "impersonal" and have no direct interest left in people on the earth plane that you desire to go on.

Eventually, these spirits will probably progress more quickly through this work, for as they give help to those below it is also given to them, according to their needs, by higher spirits. The law of compensation works in this way even in your world, for there if love is given unselfishly, generously, and wisely it will be returned in greater measure by spirits in the higher life by thought and influence which will materialize according to the requirements of the earth plane.

Meanwhile, life is very happy here and full of interest; even the grief and pain of those you love and have left behind does not affect one in the old way, for one can see beyond the trouble of the day and know it is only for a little while.

Claude communicated that his spirit body is made of chemicals, gases, and atoms – atoms of a finer nature than one finds on the earth plane. They are held together in much the same way as the atoms of the physical body, but the spirit body does not disintegrate in the same way as the physical does, because life on the third sphere will likely be as long or much longer than the one on the earth plane.

There is something substantial about my spirit body. Suppose I had to leave the third plane and to go to the fifth, sixth, or seventh plane, for good, I mean, not for a visit. I know then my entire etheric body would undergo a change: the atoms would be of a still lighter kind, because the nearer I go to the God-force, or Life-force, the more actual Life-force there is running through my body and holding those atoms together.

Because of this greater force in the higher spheres we would require less chemical matter. On the third plane the body in the way of the chemical constituents would be very much like that of the earth plane – not so much in quantity, but the same in kind. Is it not correct that hydrogen and similar gases or chemicals can be obtained in a grosser or coarser or in a more refined state, a higher state – lighter in pressure? Our bodies are made of the extremely refined variety. ..

I understand why spirits don't return and give more about the "make-up" of the spirit world in a scientific way. There is so much that is so difficult to put into words at all, especially to have to imprint on another person who is still in the limitation of the physical body – the medium – that which to us is a great shining light – the truth. We feel it, we move in it, we breathe it; but it's too great and vast a thing to explain in an hour or so for no sooner do I start to explain one phase, than I find it leads me to have to explain another, and then another, and so on. We are nearer the Infinite than you are, and are therefore more naturally conscious of the power of the Infinite, and do not require to have it manifested in detail or in infinite form to the same extent as you do. People on the earth-plane clamour for materialization; they are not conscious of those passed over unless they can see them in some form.

We here do not often "see" Christ but we can feel and are conscious of Him all the time; but if you ask me how I know it I can't tell you...

God is not known to science, because science can't measure or classify Him. But that does not show there is no God. It is the same with many things in the spirit-world.

Any time within the next thousand years the "lighter and more refined" kind of hydrogen I told you about may be known to science but it will not be known by any name we have given it here; it will be named and classified by man when he discovers it. I called it a "kind of hydrogen" because that is, it seems to me, the nearest approach in it on the earth plane, and I must call it something that will present an idea to your mind that you can "grasp." It is a definite thing.

We don't name the particles or items of the great universal force or power that permeates and is the being of everything. It is only when it filters through to the earth plane that you divide it and discover different parts and name them.

I know these things definitely; they are not my ideas or "impressions," for I am taught them by teachers and guides from the higher spheres. A great many others here have been taught these things too, but they do not get the opportunity to get them through to friends on earth. Of course, not every one who comes over here learns these things, as some are more interested and pass their time in other ways.

Suppose a spirit here a few hundred years ago had tried to explain "electricity" or "radium" to a medium on earth; how would he have done it? I suppose, incidentally, that the medium would have been burnt as a witch, or a wizard and that would have settled the matter for the time-being. You can imagine he would have been unable to express his ideas clearly. We are still in the same predicament...

We don't learn things here in terms that you understand; we learn spiritual things, which are necessary to us, for we are of the spirit world, and to find out things in your world we have to work in your conditions. Communication with me is so easy to you. I don't think you realize the "great gulf" that divides us.

In spite of the difficulties in communication, Claude further attempted to explain God to his mother. He pointed out that our finite minds cause us to think of God in a finite shape or form, as a man, because man is the highest experience of life manifest. However, he again stressed that such an image of God is very limiting.

The mind of God is operating through the various spheres on to the earth plane. It is almost as if a picture were thrown from a lantern first on to the seventh sphere; God projects his thoughts on to it, and those there get every thought, wish, desire, of God. It is as clear to them as if it were photographed on the atmosphere around them, so wherever they turn they know what God wants them to do. These "pictures" or thoughts of God seem to be composed of millions of "rays" of which you are not cognizant on earth. On the sixth sphere, the picture is like a copy of the seventh, not quite so sharp in outline or detail, and so on, slightly decreasing in clarity and sharpness from sphere to sphere, till it gets to the first sphere, where it is much fainter, because it is so close to the earth plane. On the earth plane it is faint indeed; but there, man, who has greater power if he chooses to use it, could reproduce that picture if he put himself in the right mental and spiritual condition to do so. It has to be redeveloped by man's attitude toward it. That's what I mean by saying we can interpret God if we choose. Man is given the power to see God's ways and wishes if he will put aside his lower self for a little while.

The guide who is teaching me said it is important for people to develop psychically as a step on to the higher or spiritual side. Before people can become "psychic" properly they must develop physically and mentally, too.

You say, "Mediums are often uneducated." Yes, they do not satisfy in consequence, but by their mediumship they are a bit better than they would have been without it. Still, I am not saying what is *possible*, but what is *best*.

People must learn to control the physical, the lower, or what is called "animal" part of them, and not give way to temper, greed, sensuality, jealousy, and so forth; they must cultivate the spirit, the higher or God part, the "higher self."

Claude told his mother that her spirit can see him now, but she doesn't realize it because the spirit mind can't link up with her brain. Her brain, he explained, is concentrating on what she is doing, not on seeing him.

Your conscious mind is operating through your brain. To be "developed" means you have gained such control over your body and brain that you are able to detach yourself from undesirable things and thoughts. It is this power a person sits to try and develop by quiet concentration and prayer. You see how necessary it is to get complete control, so as to command the nature of the thoughts, to be able to lift the "lower self" to meet the higher.

You could not do it always, of course, but you have to use the physical brain for material things, and to protect the physical body from enemies. For instance, if you saw a man coming for you to hit you with a brick, it would be no use to stop to think beautiful thoughts; you would have to do something and pretty quickly!

By a few moments of conscious practice every day, people can raise themselves so as to learn to "link on" or connect their minds and spirits, the lower and higher selves. The more and oftener they do it, the easier it becomes, so that in a little time there is a kind of semi-consciousness of that beautiful state helping them always.

The power you get by this "linking on" to the higher self has a great effect, not only on your own physical or lower self but on other people's too; that shows that if the majority could believe and practice this, there would be no such thing as war or enmity on the earth plane. It creates almost a tangible state or feeling.

It is the power given by the continual drawing down into the physical organism of the bit of the infinite that is in themselves, and because it is infinite it has infinite power, much greater than physical power; it is personality or temperament.

God is an impersonal personality. He is a personality of good, the personification of it, but impersonally good. "Why call Him personal at all?" I call God that because He sends out certain forces or power, but He expects them to return. Suppose we think of people as little ships sent out on the sea of life by God from his Harbour. His thought goes to each one, "May you return to Me," and the little ship goes out.

Again, to speak of the God-force and try to explain more about it. It's a mind that permeates everything. Next to being a mind it's an organism of forces – all the forces or energy or power ever known or to be known. God's mind controls everything -- all the forces in the Universe.

Returning to the spirit body, Claude talked about the aura, saying that it looks kind of like a "halo," as painters of old depicted, except that it surrounds the whole body and not just the head. He explained that it is an emanation from a body to which spirit is still attached and in-terpenetrates the surface of the body, calling it a dissemination of the spirit over the body.

The aura is of various sizes and colours and parti-colours, and is always in movement and changes in the same person at different times, for it is affected by emotion, character, and health. Intellect and intelligence determine the shape, for there is a fine head aura round anyone who is well-developed mentally.

Spirits can tell by looking at the aura if a person is psychic; that is how they know a medium, and come to them when they want to communicate with people on earth.

I think the aura goes to make up the spirit body for when the physical body dies there is no aura. In dying, the aura gets gradually less and is drawn inward and upward. I have noticed many times, for I have seen many men die on the battlefield, that at the same rate at which the aura absorbs into the body the spirit begins coming out of the head.

I think also the fact that it is possible to put all the aura on one side of the body under certain circumstances, shows it is soul. If it were only connected with the physical, it would only disappear as the body grew cold at death.

The soul, too, when out of the body looks like the aura, which does not totally disappear till the spirit and body are severed. At a materialization séance you can see the same substance as the aura coming from the body of the medium; meanwhile the aura greatly reduces.

The physical "door" of the spirit, which it uses to enter and leave the body while it sleeps, is below the ribs in front, pretty nearly the centre of the body; at death, when it leaves for good, it comes out of the head.

When the spirit is going to travel, the aura apparently sinks into the body en masse, and a strong column of "spirit-matter" comes from the door I have just spoken of. It "builds up" or shapes into the spirit body, and is connected with the physical one by a cord. In the case of a spiritually and mentally developed person, the spirit can travel a long way for the cord would be more pliable and elastic than in the case of anyone who was not developed in these respects.

Though you don't know it, it is through a person's aura you "sense" them. It is a sure indication of character, and the colours which indicate characteristics are the same as I mentioned before in another connection: blue and violet (certain shades) for spirituality; yellow and orange intellectuality; pink indicates an affectionate nature; an apple-green a well balanced mentality. The undesirable colours are certain shades of grey and brown, murky reds, and greens, which indicate sensuality, jealousy, and other unpleasant traits.

Of course there are tremendous varieties in "auras" ; they are naturally as varied as the people in the world, in shades of colour, in combination of colours, shapes, and sizes; also, in some people they are clear and well defined, while in others they are uneven, almost "sagging" or "lumpy-looking," or misty.

When any organ of the physical body is out of order or diseased, the aura in that spot dwindles for the time being; for this reason a clairvoyant can sometimes locate illness.

Claude's mother asked him to explain the difference between "astrals" and "thought-forms," to which he replied that they are quite different, and by no means interchangeable terms even though some people seem to think they are the same thing.

There are two kinds of "astrals," so called because they are functioning on the Astral plane. First, there are the spirits existing there in their astral bodies, which are made out of actual atoms. The astral, though, fine in comparison with the physical body, is still coarse, for it is only undeveloped people who are not spiritually evolved who live on that sphere. There is a great difference between it and the bodies of those on the third sphere.

There is no "death" after you leave earth, but this further difference in degrees makes people think sometimes one has to undergo that ordeal again on going higher through the different planes. This is not so, though a great change certainly does take place in the "astral body"; the chemical condition alters, it becomes refined, but is no greater than that which takes place in your earth body continually, all the cells of which change and renew several times in the course of your life there, though you are not conscious of it in either case.

When a man in the astral changes mentally, his body changes too in sympathy with his development, and in corresponding degree, but more quickly than with you.

If a man longs to progress very fast, and makes up his mind and concentrates on it, he can change in a very short time, but if he makes no special effort, and progresses slowly mentally, his body changes slowly too. This gradual refinement continues through the spheres; the change comes from within.

The second kind of astral is a spirit connected with a physical body and functioning temporarily only on the astral plane, while his earth body sleeps or is unconscious. It looks much the same as the other, but its body is actually different, for it has an astral "husk" only, much on the same principle as the temporary body made for a materializing spirit at a séance, and like that composed of astral atoms consolidated. These astral atoms collect round the aura of a developed man, and on his soul emerging from the centre of his body, these atoms close round his spirit and form a "husk" or covering to protect it in its travels.

He could not function in his real "astral" body for that is not complete; it is not complete for a curious reason. It is this: that a certain amount of the material that makes his astral body is not available while he is connected with his physical body, for it goes to make the vital cord or connection between his travelling spirit and his stationary body, which is only severed at death.

After this has occurred, of course, no cord being then required, this material is available for his astral body, and so he no longer requires to borrow astral atoms to protect himself; his spirit is sufficiently clothed, being complete. As I am not in the astral, I find it difficult to tell if a person is in their astral body or not.

This accounts too for the difficulty a clairvoyant sometimes has in being able to say if a person is in or out of their physical body permanently. They, too, are, it must be remembered, seeing in conditions other than their normal. Sight varies enough even on the earth plane; no two men see exactly alike.

If you took a collection of people to a hill top and asked them to describe the view without artificial aid they would all see in different degrees: some only things near, others only things distant, some as it were through a haze and others clearly. This is why normal clairvoyance is often incorrect - things are difficult to see in the right perspective; and it varies too according to the bias of the medium's brain on which it is registered by the sight.

A "thought-form" is a picture, a thought-photograph, projected through the atmosphere by some one, but the recipient would have to mentally "develop" it, as it were, in order to see it; by that I mean they would have to be thinking of the sender at the right moment, and in the right way. Space is nothing, for it takes no longer to think four or five hundred miles than into the next room. So if you are in the right mental condition you can see a thought-form; it's only a picture in the atmosphere.

This explains certain things; for instance visions of Christ to the dying. Hundreds on the battlefield may see Him individually and spontaneously. If He is projecting His thought to all who are lying there, all who are attuned in mind can and may be able to see Him. Just as when a ship at sea sends out a wireless message or a call for help, it is not confined to one receiver, but is open to all ships and receiving stations which are suitably attuned. So all who are suitably attuned and harmonized can receive thought pictures, impressions, and inspiration. This explains also how various people in widely separated places may simultaneously be "inspired" by one individual. "Inspired," I said, not "controlled," remember, Mum; that is a very different matter. Personally, I don't believe spirits from the higher spheres ever "control" people on earth. It is hard enough for us who are only on the third sphere to get back into the old conditions, for those it would be exceedingly difficult and a deliberate waste; it would be like engaging a tutor of the highest scholastic attainments to teach an infant its A B C's!

Now as regards a so-called "ghost" haunting a particular spot: If it is a persistent haunt that has continued for many years even for centuries, it is almost certainly a thought-form and not a spirit; for it is very unlikely that any spirit would be so unfriended as to be permitted to go on in this aimless and unhappy manner indefinitely for as soon as anyone desires help here it is forthcoming.

What happens is this. Certain events, probably tragic, which are felt very intensely by the participants at the time, leave a very clear-cut and well-defined picture in the atmosphere, and at first for a short time the actors in the scene may return in spirit to the spot, and by thinking over what happened revivify and intensify that thought picture. Ordinary people then come to that place knowing its history, and some may see the "ghost," and they see it because they are psychic and unconsciously psychometrize the atmosphere and so mentally develop the picture that is there, and to constantly renew the image, which thus becomes almost permanent. Yes, I know it does seem difficult to realize, but it also applies to "feeling" as well as "seeing" past conditions; thus a medium feels pain and discomfort when describing the illness of anyone. The medium is psychometrizing the condition connected with the spirit while it was in a body, and not the spirit itself.

I say this because I have been told and have noticed myself that spirits are surprised on returning to earth to hear themselves described with symptoms of disease they have almost forgotten they ever suffered. For instance, your father, who "died" over thirty-five years ago here, is in perfect health, yet, whenever he returns to earth the mediums describe him as having a cough, and discomfort in his chest; that was true when he passed over (he died of pneumonia), but of course is totally unlike his present condition.

Another man I know, who had some very painful disease which affected one leg, tells me he gets quite angry when he hears it described now, as he no longer feels it at all even when he returns to earth conditions, and yet, the mediums describe it most accurately, and one might imagine he was still in suffering instead of in perfect health.

Claude told his mother that he wanted to impress upon her the enormous importance of thought. He explained that they should be guarded as carefully as deeds, as a thought can impress an image on the surrounding atmosphere, leaving a permanent record. Thoughts alone can haunt people after they die, even if a negative thought was not actually carried out.

In the spirit world, too, we can speak by thought, by telepathy; that is how we overcome the difficulty of different languages. This does not mean that I have no privacy of thought, and that my mind is open to all to read. I have to project a thought when I want to communicate it, just as all a hypnotist's thoughts are not conveyed to his patients, but only those which he directly impresses. If you would get people "attuned" properly, they could even think music at each other!

All wrong thought goes to build up and strengthen the power of evil – called by men the devil. In the beginning, I am told it was almost negative; man increased it himself by inflicting pain, by cruelty, by lust and envy.

There is great spiritual and mental "unrest" among men now and has been for some time past; however, undefined, obscure, and misunderstood, because man is evolving and there is an unconscious struggle between the spiritual and animal in him. Chaos and disturbance are the result.

As to the people whose "faith" you say is "shaken" by the war, all I can say is, it's not much of a faith! They are trying to limit God again; He does not work for one country, but for the good of all mankind, and each nation will learn what it requires for its future development. It would be as sensible for a doctor to treat one symptom of disease in the body only, instead of strengthening and cleansing the whole of it. The systems of the world are being purified. In the past we have put aside or trifled with things that now must be faced in earnest.

The earth plane is God's garden, and it was a beautiful garden; what is left of God in it is still beautiful, but it is now full of weeds of evil, disease, poverty, and selfishness.

The gardeners are beginning to realize that further trimming is of no use, and these things must be uprooted utterly. In the past so many enjoyed the sunshine and fruit and flowers, and neglected the weeds, which were brushed aside and hidden as unlovely and troublesome things; they have now become rampant, and only drastic measures are of any use.

I know sometimes things look depressing, but I solemnly promise you there is a silver lining to this dark cloud. Men in the old days worked for individual progress; in the future, the ideal will be to work for others, for the good of the whole and the improvement of the community.

I am told the sacrifices of this war have not been in vain; that a purified England will result. There will be a spiritual revolution; people will try to face truth, to drop some of the shams that are now used to veil it. Perhaps present events do seem to you a "dark tunnel," but I see the sun shining at the end of it, and I know there has never been a crisis in the world's history which has held so much certainty of ultimate good arising out of it.

Nations and peoples, like individuals, sooner or later reap what they themselves have sown of good and evil; and knowing this, one realizes that no life, nor the life of any one nation is a succession of disconnected events. There is a sequence running though them all. They fit into each other like the pieces of a puzzle, though one only sees it clearly as a whole when life on earth is over and the last piece has been fitted into its place.

In the Preface to the second book, Mrs. Kelway-Bamber states that while most of the messages came through Mrs. Leonard, she began receiving messages herself via automatic writing. She pointed out that due to the limitations of language, which is inadequate to express spiritual matters, the words used throughout the talks by Claude are the "nearest equivalent" to whatever Claude was trying to express, explain, or describe. Some of Claude's talk on the difficulties of mediumship are set forth in the Introduction of this book. Below are extracts from the second book.

Advanced Teachings: You say some people think my theories are very advanced for the third sphere. Well, darling, though I am living there, I frequently go to the higher spheres for special instruction, for, as I told you a long time ago, I am being trained as a teacher, and have already begun my work. I was chosen for this because I was peculiarly suited for it, and not because I was in any way "better" or even as good as many beautiful spirits here. We will take my old simile, and consider God in the light of the "Great Headmaster" this time. The different spheres are the different classes or forms of His school, the seventh as the highest. The minds there are very advanced and in consequence learn a good deal from the Headmaster Himself; they are sufficiently educated to appreciate and understand His teaching. Those in the sixth are instructed by teachers from the seventh and so on down the different spheres, the pupils in each being taught according to their development and requirements. The source of knowledge is one and the same, only it is suited by the teachers to the various grades and degrees. The earth is the most elementary. Certain spirits, of which I am one, who are required for special work, are sent to the higher spheres from the third for particular teaching... I find learning is easy; the difficulty lies in remembering and projecting my thoughts through the medium when I come to earth. I cannot dwell therefore on the wonder, glory, and importance of the things I tell you as I should like to do.

Spirit Travel: For traveling under particular conditions we have to learn to control the forces and powers within ourselves so as to be able to go through certain experiences. A novice is only allowed to walk about here as if he were on the earth; if he has to go on a journey, guides go with him in order to protect him – in fact, they have to work and concentrate on him to keep him "intact" during his voyage through space! If a newcomer took himself from here to the earth plane – if he could – his body would be almost falling to pieces; it would be flopping about because the currents and forces in the atmosphere would be too powerful for him. When I come to you I concentrate and will my body to stiffen and consolidate, and not until I feel I have absolute mental command over myself in detail, even down to my toes and ears, do I start. I had to learn how to locate in my mind the exact place or distance from my mind to where my toes would be, for I must set the mental picture to get exactly five toes on each foot. I must then switch off and yet retain the idea while I think of what the top of my head looks like. I do all this because as soon as I get in touch with these atmospheric forces I have to hold myself together strongly to resist them. Now, if I am not in a hurry to reach my destination, I do not trouble to do anything further than to keep a clear picture of myself in the proportions in which I appear in my own sphere, and I project my thoughts all the time to the place to which I am going, but the first consideration is always my body. If I were in a great hurry, directly I started I should get the picture of myself very clear, and then I should quickly but gradually contract my body from within; only an advanced spirit can do this, not a newcomer. I begin by drawing my whole consciousness within myself, and in so doing I draw upward and onward each part of my body, making myself very self-centered and bringing my extremities nearer to my consciousness. I have told you my body is made of atoms, but because they are minutely fine I can actually consolidate them into very small space; there is so much God-force holding them together. When I get near my destination, I gradually and consciously expand my body to normal dimensions. I only contract my body in this way for emergency traveling, and I know spirits who have been here many years and who cannot do it; it is only intended for those who have serious and special work to do, in which case it is expedient.

Apparitions: If they have first to learn how to appear, you want to know why it is that some spirits, practically at the moment of death, manage to come to people on earth. In these cases it is generally a thought-form, especially if the spirit is seen in very material conditions, such as wounded, covered with mud, in tattered clothes, etc. It might even be a thought-form not consciously projected by the spirit itself. There is always a link between the spirits of people who truly love each other, a sort of conscious telepathy, and the passing out of one under these conditions would give a "pull" or "jerk" to the spirit of the other who remained.

Subconscious Mind: The origin of the subconscious mind is that bit of God which we call spirit; it grows and only develops as subconscious mind by recording certain experiences of the physical body. The subconscious mind starts growing directly as the spirit is attached to the body. As soon as the conscious mind begins to work, it registers on the subconscious... As the subconscious is the spirit mind, it is much less limited, and registers everything even before the conscious mind can grasp it, for this operates through the brain.

Personality: Directly, as the conscious mind starts working there is will-power, and the personality begins to develop; it is largely influenced by early impressions. The subconscious mind knows its origin, and tries to safeguard and support the growing personality. It repeats continually. "I come from God – be God-like," in its endeavour to influence it. This has been called conscience.

Temptation: While developing through the body the earth conditions may tempt the personality to express itself through its lower animal senses; the will-power is there and the spirit, but the personality puts the will-power aside and shuts off the voice of the spiritual mind. A personality in its first incarnation is inclined to be animal and rather brutish, for it has had no individual experience of spirit-life, and it is feeling the sense of novelty, and is living to the full the life of the physical in which it has first awakened. As the personality grows, the spirit body grows in keeping, and in this case it would be coarse and the aura badly shaped, a spirit body suited for the lowest astral. God does not decide the quality of the spirit-body. Man himself does.

Hauntings: In the astral, this personality is in a stupid state because it is undeveloped except in a physical sense, so that when cut off from the earth-body it feels lost. In a genuine haunting, the personality is so unused to anything but the physical, it hangs about in a blind unreasoning manner; it can't understand or think in its new state, and wants to move about in a mechanical way in the old conditions which it recognizes. It can only do so for a time, because that bit of God is tugging it, and it is bound to prevail in the end, however long it takes, because the new body, the astral, though still coarse, is more akin in the spirit than the old one; therefore, it will be drawn to the place to which it belongs eventually.

Happy Materialists: You say you know some people who think of nothing but material things, and yet seem perfectly happy and have all that heart can desire. Apparently, yes, but not really, for material things alone cannot suffice for long. That "little bit of God" within is tireless; it will keep on tugging continually, and so there is always something wanting – an emptiness, an unrest, that is ever there, however carefully it may be concealed. Why do you suppose so many people who have much of the world's goods gamble, drink or live fast lives? They want to drown this feeling of "emptiness," for they are not prepared to sacrifice or risk anything even though on the whole, life has not brought them all they hoped and expected from it under the circumstances. Life is made up of comparisons; it is a continual comparing of extremes. The materialist envies the spiritual man, who, he recognizes, has found an anodyne for that irrepressible discontent, and the spiritual man envies the materialist not because he desires his worldly possessions for himself, but because he feels they might be so great a power for good if used aright. These extremes are only extremes in so far as men make them so. There is no reason at all why a man should not be thoroughly versed in material and practical things and be thoroughly spiritual too. They are not meant to be antagonistic, but like different notes in a chord, are intended to blend and make one a perfect and harmonious whole.

Cultivation: Many people are imperfectly developed – a genius who is not spiritual, or an idealist who is not practical. They have each a side missing, and they will not realize the best in life till they cultivate that side. The soul is like a rough diamond, the beauty of which is concealed till it is out and polished. The earth is the workshop in which the cutting and polishing will be done. It is easier to be good and to know what is right than man realizes, for the little bit that connects him with God is always tugging at him, and he does not understand he can get all he wants if he will only "link up" to receive it.

Balance: The danger lies in this, that in order to develop [occult] power to this extent, a man has had to detach himself so much from material things, mental as well as physical, that he loses his sense of proportion, as to do it he must shut himself off from other people, and often becomes selfish and psychically self-centered in consequence. These occultists feel a kind of intolerance of their fellow creatures. They don't lose sympathy or pity, but they have lost the power of definite action in a material way, which makes it almost impossible for them to help others in a real, practical, or common-sense manner...If a man is wise, kind, broadminded, and unselfish, and uses this [occult] power to promote good, to succor and help others, he is safe; but otherwise it brings its own nemesis, for it leaves him suddenly not only powerless with regard to the occult force of which he has been so sure, but depleted physically and mentally. I have seen it many times.

Reincarnation: In the first place, you must understand, [the old soul] returns to earth when and if he is really desirous of doing so. The higher guides in consultation decide on a suitable environment, and then explain and discuss their reasons with him; they also give him special teaching in company with others who are ready to return also. When the time arrives and the physical body of the infant is in the early stage of its growth, the chosen spirit is sent to earth, where it remains in close juxtaposition with its future mother till by degrees the spirit becomes merged into her aura, and the "cord," which will ultimately connect the spirit with its new body, forms and penetrating the mother's physical organism, attaches itself to the child. The spirit then gradually decreases in size, concentrates, as it were, and at the time of birth is suitable for the little body which it envelops and partly interpenetrates. The process is exactly the reverse in one respect to that of a new soul, which has to grow from the" drop" (spark) I told you about, but is analogous in every other respect.

Christ: Here we never trouble to think and wonder if Christ was born of a virgin or not, etc., but we know the events connected with His physical body do not matter at all. It was the *God in Him* that was the great moving power that has carried His teaching so far over the world, because, being of God, it touched the God in every man who could instinctively recognize and respond to the truth.

Premonitions of Death: A spirit even when knowing its own "death" is near may not be able to get the knowledge through to its own physical brain directly, and in that case it sometimes tells some other spirit, with a view to being retold the fact itself when it is back again and fully conscious in its physical body. And when the knowledge does get through in this way, you call it premonition.

Recalling Out-of-Body Experiences: Sometimes the traveling spirit, immediately on its return to the body, tries to imprint the memory of its experiences on the brain, and these get confused with the mechanical action of which I have just spoken; the result is intermingling and incongruity. Some people, there are very few, can remember their spirit experiences and, if they are sufficiently evolved for this, their guides may tell them sometimes of impending events; some few other spirits, who find they cannot bring these memories through to their waking consciousness correctly in an elaborate or detailed way, have learnt to impress a sign or a symbol on the brain which they know will convey a certain meaning to themselves in their normal waking condition.

The Ego: When this "drop" of God-force breaks away from God to come to earth and animate a human body, part of it remains behind; this part is the "Ego," the reservoir of divinity. It is severed from the body at death, never from the spirit, for man is always connected with God; disconnection would mean annihilation. As man desires to draw from the God force, the "tube" connecting him with that strengthens and enlarges, and increases his capacity to receive it.

Twin Soul: When the "drop" of God-force that makes the spirit of man separates from God and comes to the world, it divides into halves and goes to two separate mothers and thus a boy and girl are always born from each "drop." In fact, on the earth plane, things are generally constituted with a "counterpart," an opposite; they are male and female, positive and negative. The union of these creates the proper balance and produces something. The positive is described as the transmitter, the negative as the receiver; at a séance for materialization the medium places the sitters alternately, positive and negative, in order to produce something physical. Certain plants are positive and negative, and it is their union by fertilization which produces the fruit; it is the mingling of the sun and rain which makes conditions for growth and health of vegetation. Man often forgets the necessity for this ideal mating within himself in order to produce character; he sometimes goes to extremes and becomes too positive or too negative, and thus loses balance and upsets the harmony necessary for ideal production.

Harmony: When the mental is absolutely dominant, you get a selfish, calculating, cold-blooded person; if the physical dominates the mental, you get sensuality. When a man learns to control and harmonize, and balance the two, his spirit gets its opportunity and you have a splendid man, a "whole" man. There is another alternative: sometimes the spirit tries to control before this ideal state is reached, and then in the man there is a struggle, a dual personality.

CHAPTER FOUR

THOMAS

Background: *The story of Private Thomas Dowding was received by means of the automatic writing form of mediumship by Wellesley Tudor Pole and told in a popular 1917 book entitled "Private Dowding."*

In the Introduction, Tudor Pole, an Englishman, states that on March 12, 1917, he was walking by the sea when he felt the presence of someone. He looked around and saw no one. However, he continued to feel throughout the day that someone was trying to communicate with him. That evening, while visiting a clairvoyant lady, he was told that a man dressed in khaki was sitting on the chair near him. She described him as mature looking, with a small moustache, and appearing somewhat sad. Upon arriving home, Tudor Pole sat down at his writing table and with the pen in his hand began to write in an "involuntary sort of way." He said the thoughts were not his own, the language a little unusual, and some of the ideas not in accord with his own knowledge or beliefs. He felt that some intelligence outside of himself was speaking through his mind and his pen.

Born in 1884, Tudor Pole became, at age 20, the managing director of a family business involving grains and cereals. He traveled extensively in the marketing of that business. During World War I, he served as an officer in the Directorate of Military Intelligence for Great Britain. In the years following the Great War, Tudor Pole gained a reputation as a personal guide, healer, philosopher, medium, and mystic. Other books authored by him include "The Silent Road," "Writing on the Ground," "My Dear Alexias," and "A Man Seen Afar."

While "Thomas Dowding" is a pseudonym of a soldier that Tudor Pole did not know personally, the sincerity of the story along with Tudor

Pole's reputation compelled many readers to accept it as a true story. "His whole philosophy is a gentle, insistent, assertion that the life we know is only a minute part of a greater continuum, existing far back and far ahead," wrote D. F. O. Russell of Tudor Pole in the Foreword to "Writing on the Ground."

Russell continued: "Tudor Pole's ability to scan this continuum brings glimpses that are denied to most of us. Through this facility or power of access and by the faculties incidental to it, he lifts a curtain on parts of the New Testament story long obscured. The process throws up ideas at once old and new, at once strange and yet familiar: ideas that have a haunting nostalgia suggesting that they are related to something we have always known – perhaps without realising that we knew."

Tudor Pole wrote: "To me, my communication with Thomas Dowding was so real that he seemed to be in the room sitting at my elbow, prompting my pen. I know there have been many books written containing messages said to be handed down from another plane of existence. One cannot doubt the possibility of "spirit communication," as it is often called. It seems to me that there can be no final proof concerning these matters. One must be guided by the interior worth of the messages themselves. I tell you, for instance, that I am satisfied I have been speaking with a soldier who was killed in battle seven months ago. I have set down the experience in writing exactly as it has come to me. I cannot, however, prove the genuineness of the experience to anyone else. I cannot even prove it finally to myself."

Novelist Rosamond Lehmann became friends with Tudor Pole during the last six years of his life. "Who was the man known to his many friends at TP?" she asked. "I don't know; no one, presumably, will ever know, except for certain fellow initiates and Elder Brothers. Obviously, he was a Master: an incomparable Seer, infinitely adept in out-of-the-body traveling; also an 'ordinary man' with wide business interests, an Intelligence officer in World War I, lover of animals, and of trees: a man with a practical interest in archaeological research and a surprising grasp of alchemy and ecology. He warned repeatedly of the threats of planetary pollution many years before this became the subject of general concern. In short, a man of formidable authority, as enigmatic as he was accessible."

Reader alert: *The automatic writing form of mediumship is discussed in the Introduction of this book. Words below in standard print are those of Private Dowding, as recorded by Tudor Pole. Words in italics* *are those of the editor of this book. The first message was recorded on March 12, 1917.*

✳✳✳

I am grateful for the opportunity. You may not realise how much some of us long to speak to those we have left behind. It is not easy to get messages through with certainty. They are so often lost in transit or misinterpreted. Sometimes the imagination of the receiver weaves a curious fabric round the thoughts we try to pass down, then the ideas we want to communicate are either lost or disfigured.

I was a schoolmaster in a small East Coast town before the war. I was an orphan, somewhat of a recluse, and I made friends but slowly. My name is of no importance; apparently names over here are not needed. I became a soldier in the autumn of 1915, and left my narrow village life behind. These details, however, are really of no importance. They may act as a background to what I have to say. I joined as a private and died as a private. My soldiering lasted just nine months, eight of which were spent training in Northumberland. I went out with my battalion to France in July 1916, and we went into the trenches almost at once. I was killed by a shell splinter one evening in August, and I believe that my body was buried the following day. As you see, I hasten over these unimportant events, important to me once, but now of no real consequence. How we overestimate the significance of earthly happenings! One only realizes this when freed from earthly ties.

Well, my body soon became cannon fodder, and there were few to mourn me. It was not for me to play anything but an insignificant part in the world tragedy which is still unfolding.

I am still myself, a person of no importance, but I feel I should like to say a few things before passing along. I feared death, but then that was natural. I was timid and even feared life and its pitfalls. So I was afraid of being killed and was sure it would mean extinction. There are still many who believe that. It is because extinction has not come to me that I want to speak to you. May I describe my experiences? Perhaps they may prove useful to some. How necessary that some of us should speak back across the border! The barriers must be broken down. This is one of the ways of doing it. Listen therefore to what I have to say.

Physical death is nothing. There really is no cause for fear. Some of my pals grieved for me. When I "went West" they thought I was dead for good. This is what happened. I have a perfectly clear memory of the whole incident. I was waiting in the corner of a traverse to go on guard. It was a fine evening. I had no special intimation of danger, until I heard the whizz of a shell. Then followed an explosion somewhere behind me. I crouched down involuntarily, but was too late. Something struck hard, hard, hard, against my neck. Shall I ever lose the memory of that hardness? It is the only unpleasant incident that I can remember. I fell, and as I did so, without passing through any apparent interval of unconsciousness, I found myself outside myself. You will learn to know what a small incident this dying is.

Think of it! One moment I was alive, in the earthly sense, looking over a trench parapet, unalarmed, normal. Five seconds later I was standing outside my body, helping my pals to carry my body down the trench labyrinth towards a dressing station. They thought I was senseless but alive. I did not know whether I had jumped out of my body through shell shock, temporarily or forever. You see what a small thing is death, even the violent death of war! I seemed in a dream! I had dreamt that someone or something had knocked me down. Now I was dreaming that I was outside of my body. Soon I would wake up and find myself in the traverse waiting to go on guard...It all happened so simply. Death for me was a simple experience – no horror, no long-drawn suffering, no conflict. It comes to many in the same way. My pals need not fear death. Few of them do; nevertheless there is an underlying dread of possible extinction. I dreaded that; many soldiers do, but they rarely have time to think about such things. As in my case, thousands of soldiers pass over without knowing it. If there be shock, it is not the shock of physical death. Shock comes later when comprehension dawns. Where is my body? Surely, I am not dead. In my own case I know nothing more than I have already related at the time. When I found that my two pals could carry my body without my help, I drooped behind. I just followed in a curiously humble way. Humble? Yes, because I seemed so useless. We met a stretcher party. My body was hoisted on to the stretcher. I wondered when I should get back with it again. You see, I was so little dead that I imagined that I was still physically alive. Think of it for a moment before we pass on. I had been struck by a shell splinter. There was no pain. The life was knocked out of my body; again, I say, there was no pain.

Then I found that the whole of myself – all, that is, that thinks and sees and feels, and knows – was still alive and conscious. I had begun a new chapter of life. I will tell you what I felt like. It was as if I had been running hard, until hot and breathless. I had thrown my overcoat away. The coat was my body, and if I had not thrown it away I should have been suffocated. I cannot describe the experience in any other way: there is nothing else to describe.

My body went to the first dressing station, and after examination was taken to a mortuary. I stayed near it all that night, watching, but without thought. It was as if my being, feeling, and thinking had become suspended by some power outside myself. The sensation came over me gradually as the night advanced. I still expected to wake up in my body again – that is, so far as I expected anything. Then I lost consciousness and slept soundly.

When Thomas awoke, his body had disappeared and he began hunting for it. He continued to feel as if in a dream and would soon awaken. As soon as he stopped looking for it, the realization came that he had been killed. He felt a sudden freedom and lightness, as if his being had expanded. He felt he was in a body of some kind, but he couldn't picture it. He began to feel as if he were floating above the battlefield in a mist that muffled sounds and blurred the vision.

It was like looking through the wrong end of a telescope. Everything was distant, minute, misty, unreal. Guns were being fired. It might all have been millions of miles away. The detonation hardly reached me. I was conscious of the shells bursting without actually seeing them. The ground seemed very empty. No soldiers were visible. It was like looking down from above the clouds, yet that doesn't exactly express it either. When a shell that took life exploded, then the sensation of it came much nearer to me. The noise and tumult came over the border with the lives of the slain. A curious way of putting it. All this time I was very lonely. I was conscious of none near me. I was neither in the world of matter, nor could I be sure I was in any place at all. Just simply conscious of my own existence in a state of dream. I think I fell asleep for the second time, and long remained unconscious and in a dreamless condition.

At last I awoke. Then a new sensation came to me. It was as if I stood on a pinnacle, all that was essential of me. The rest receded, receded, receded. All appertaining to bodily life seemed to be drooping away down into a bottomless abyss. There was no feeling of irretrievable loss. My being seemed both minute and expansive at the same time. All that was not really me slipped down and away. The sense of loneliness deepened.

Thomas pointed out that there were difficulties in communicating, explaining that he was impressing ideas on Tudor Pole's brain and those ideas were then whirled around in Tudor Pole's mind and expressed in Tudor Pole's words, not necessarily the words that he (Thomas) would have used. While he could not see Tudor Pole's pen or the words put down on paper, he could see if Tudor Pole was getting the ideas.

I can see your mind freely because I see you have deliberately chained your imagination, and so I can impress you freely and clearly. From this you may notice that I am a little further along my new road. I have been helped. Also I have recovered from the shock, not of my transition but of my recognition of it. This is no subtlety; it is simply what I mean. I am no longer alone – I have met my dear brother. He came out here three years ago and has come down to welcome me. The tie between us is strong. William could not get near me for a long time, he says. The atmosphere was so thick He hoped to reach me in time to avert the shock to which I have referred, but found it impossible. He is working among the newly arrived and has wide experience.

A good deal of what follows came to me from him. I have made it my own, and so can pass it on. You see, I am still possessed with the desire to make my experience, my adventure, of help to others who have not yet arrived here. It appears that there are rest halls in this region, especially prepared for newly arrived pilgrims. I shall use your language. We can only convey our experiences approximately. To describe conditions here in words is quite impossible. Please remember this. My brother helped me into one of those rest halls. Confusion at once dropped away from me. Never shall I forget my happiness. I sat in the alcove of a splendid domed hall. The splashing of a fountain reached my tired being and soothed me. The fountain played music, colour, harmony, bliss. All discordances vanished and I was at peace. My brother sat near me. He could not stay long, but promised to return...

I am beginning to meet people and to exchange ideas. Strange that the only person I came across for a long time was my brother. He tells me that I have never been really alone. The mist around me, shifting me off, has emanated from myself, he says. This fact rather humiliates me. I supposed my loneliness of life and character whilst on earth have followed me here. I always lived in books, they were my real world. And even then, any reading was technical rather than general.

I begin to see now that my type of mind would find itself isolated, or rather would emanate isolation, when loosed from earthly trammels.

I shall remain near earth conditions, whilst learning lessons I refused to learn before.

It is dangerous to live to and for oneself. Tell this to my fellows with emphasis. The life of a recluse is unwise, except for the very few who have special work that requires complete silence and isolation. I was not one of these. I cannot remember doing anything really worthwhile. I never looked outside myself.

My school? Well, teaching bored me. I simply did it to earn my bread and cheese. People will say I was unique, a crabby, selfish old bachelor. Selfish, yes, but alas! far from being unique. I was thirty-seven when I came over here – that is, my body was. Now I feel so ignorant and humble that I don't feel I've begun to have any age at all.

I must dwell on this. Live widely. Don't get isolated. Exchange thoughts and services. Don't read too much. That was my mistake. Books appealed to me more than life or people. I am now suffering for my mistakes. In passing on these details of my life I am hoping to free myself.

What a good thing the war; it dragged me out into life. In those nine months, I learned more about human nature than I had conceived possible. Now I am learning about my poor fossilized old self. It is a blessing I came here...

Tell people to control their worldly interests from outside. If you identify yourself heart and soul with some material project or under-taking, you will find it hanging on to you over here. It will obsess you, blot out the view, make progress impossible...Take a bird's-eye dispassionate view of all your worldly interests. Master them or they will master you. In the latter case, when you get here you will be miserable. Life will seem empty, a wilderness. Earth ties will tighten that grip, yet you will be unable to respond. Confusion will result – that is purgatory.

There are many forms. Each of us creates his own purgatorial condition. If I had my time over again, how different I should live my life! I was not one of those who lived solely for the purpose of satisfying ambition. Money was a secondary consideration. Yes, I erred in the other extreme, for I neither lived enough among my fellow men nor interested myself in their affairs. Well, I have created my own purgatory. I must live through it somehow. Good night. I will return again.

Thomas concluded that he was in a state of consciousness not far removed from earth conditions, but that he was journeying forward to a wider, truer life. He said he had no right to speak with any authority and questioned whether he was in a state of illusion. Nevertheless, everything seemed just as real to him as it did when he was on the earth plane, even more real. However, because he wasn't sure he was speaking with authority he felt it best to cease communicating with Tudor Pole. He returned two days later, informing Tudor Pole that a guide told him that he was too hasty in cutting off communication.

He did not think there would be much harm if I kept the channel open a little longer. He impressed on me the importance of reminding you that the conditions now around me are impermanent, and to that extent, unreal. From his standpoint the value of such messages as these depend upon the emphasis placed on this fact: The spiritual world is everywhere. The life of spirit is eternal, perfect, supreme. We humans hide from the light. We grovel among the illusions created by our thoughts. We surround ourselves with misconceptions. We refuse to rise into the Christ Sphere. The Christ Sphere is everywhere, and yet, by some strange paradox, we were able to shut it out from view. All these thoughts were new to me. I begin to see what is meant. If I did not do so, I could not pass the ideas on. You say these thoughts are quite familiar to you. I am surprised at this. What a little world I have been living in...

I have looked into hell. I may have to return to that region. I shall be given my choice. Grant that I may be strong enough to offer myself freely. Hell is a thought region. Evil dwells there and works out its purposes. The forces used to hold mankind down in the darkness of ignorance are generated in hell. It is not a place; it is a condition. It has taken millions of years to reach its present state. I dare not tell you what I saw there. My brother needed help. A soldier had been killed who had committed very evil deeds. I will draw a veil over them. He was a degenerate, a murderer, a sensualist. He died cursing God and man. An awful death. This man was drawn toward hell by the law of attraction. My brother had been sent off to rescue him. He took me with him. At first I refused to go. Then I went...An angel of light came to protect us, otherwise we should have been lost in the blackness of the pit. This sounds sensational, even grotesque. It is the truth...

The power of evil! Have you any idea of its mighty strength, its lure? Can that power be an illusion too? The angel said so. The angel said the power of hell was now at its supreme height. It drew its power from man. As man rose toward spiritual life the powers of darkness would subside and finally become extinguished. Extinguished is my word.

The angel said "transmuted." That conception is quite beyond me. We descended gloomy avenues. The darkness grew. There was a strange allurement about the atmosphere. Even the angel's light grew dim. I thought we were lost. At moments I hoped we were lost. So strong is the attraction. I cannot understand it. Something sensual within me leaped and burned. I thought I had emptied myself of self before undertaking this great adventure. Had I done so, I should have been safe. As it was, I should have been lost but for the angel's and my brother's help. I felt the giant lusts of the human race. They thrilled through me. I could not keep them out. We descended deeper. I say "descended." If hell is not a place, how can one "descend"? I asked my brother. He said we were not moving in the physical sense. Our progress depended on certain thought processes evoked by the Will.

Thomas found it all very strange, but the angel told him not to dwell on what he saw in the dark regions. In fact, Thomas was not able to go all the way to where the rescue was attempted. The angel and his brother left him behind in what seemed to him like a dark forest. He felt stagnation everywhere. His brother told him that people who die filled with thoughts of selfishness and sensuality go to this area. They meet a degree of darkness that is the counterpart of their own interior condition. They are led to believe that the unreal is the real.

The race will never rise to greatness until the passions are controlled. This refers to nations and individuals. On earth I was never interested in such matters. I did not realise the existence of the sexual canker at the heart of human life. What a terrible thing this is! Do not wait until you come over here. Set to work at once. There is no time to lose. Gain control of self. Then retain control by emptying yourself of self. All the thoughts of lust and passion, greed, hatred, envy, and, above all, selfishness, passing through the minds of men and women generate the condition called hell. Purgatory and hell are different states. We all must pass through a purging, purifying process after leaving the earth life. I am still in purgatory. Some day I shall rise above it. The majority who come over here rise above or rather through purgatory into higher conditions. A minority fail to relinquish their thoughts and beliefs in the pleasures of sin and the reality of the sense life. They sink by the weight of their own thoughts. No outside power can attract a man against his will. A man sinks or rises through the action of a spiritual law of gravity. He is never safe until he has emptied himself completely. You see

how I emphasize this fact, Some of these thoughts came to me while I
waited in the gloomy forest. Then the angel and my brother returned.
They had found him for whom they sought. He would not come away.
They had to leave him there. Fear held him. He said his existence was
awful, but he was afraid to move for fear worse conditions befell.

Fear chained him. No outside power can unchain that man. Release
will come from within someday. Sadly we returned to our own places.
I began to realise what power King Fear holds over nearly all of us. The
angel said that fear would be destroyed when love comes into her own.
He said the time was coming. I have much to think about. I am going
into the Hall of Silence. If I can return again, I will. Goodbye.

*When Thomas returned, he said that the war, he was informed, was
"an outward manifestation of the powers of evil in their attempt to ob-
struct the inflow of light." At least, that is what he was told, though he
could not completely understand it. He added that it was not his intent
to teach or preach, especially since he was still floundering in his attempt
to adjust to his new environment. He simply felt an obligation to pass on
his experiences, reiterating that people should not fear death.*

I want to say a few words about love – very few, because I know so
little. Also because love is spoken about too much already, whereas it
should be *lived*. If you would dwell in peace, learn to love deeply. Never cease from loving. Jesus said a good deal about love, if I remember
rightly. Look up what he said, and *live it*.

Love God by pouring yourself away. Love your fellows by giving
them all you possess of light and truth. Love love for its own blessed
sake. Such love will bring you nearer heaven.

I have spoken about illusion several times. I return to it once more. I begin to see that phenomenal existence, whether on earth or here, is so impermanent as to be unreal. This is hard saying. I do not yet understand it.

Live above those conditions which, after much meditation, appear
to you to be illusory. That is the best advice I can give.

The Messenger has spoken several times about evil. I cannot entirely shake off the effects of my visit to the lower regions, where evil
reigns as lord and king. It appears that evil is not real or permanent,
but this power can be transmitted until it serves ends that are divine.
More than this I cannot say, because I do not know. If you can realise
that evil has no real existence and can be eliminated entirely from human life, you will have learnt much. Remember what was said about

stagnation. Keep moving in some direction all the time. How was it that I lived so stagnantly while on earth? Let my life be an example.

Tudor Pole noted that Thomas could not explain why he chose him (Tudor-Pole), a total stranger, to communicate through. He also told him that the Messenger warned him against communicating with earth at all, apparently because so much of it is illusory and subject to misinterpretation or distortion. Yet, he felt impelled to communicate. While Tudor Pole pressed him for his true name, "Thomas" was unable to get it through, even though he did get "William," his brother's name, through. (See Introduction concerning the difficulty with names.) Thomas continually stressed that he was still adapting and learning and by no means was in a position to teach. (The much more complete story of Private Dowding can be found in the book by than name, now republished by White Crow Books, the publisher of this book.)

CHAPTER FIVE

ROLF

Background: *Unlike Raymond, Bob, Claude, and Thomas, Private Rolf Little did not fall on the battlefield. He died of double pneumonia as a result of crude conditions in his camp before he could join the forces on the front. Still, he was a victim of the war, and the grief felt by his mother, the author of "Rolf's Life in the Spirit World," was no less than that of other mothers.*

Although no publication year is given in the book, it appears to have been first published around 1920 by Almorris Press Ltd. of London. The author is shown simply as "His Mother," although one might infer from the contents of the book that her name was Nelly Little.

According to "Nelly," Rolf, her eldest son, was just 19 when he joined the Army right after the outbreak of the war during August 1914. He became a member of the Grenadier Guards, and was first assigned to the camp at Caterham. Due to very crowded, damp, and unsanitary living conditions there, he developed measles, followed by double pneumonia, and died on March 15, 1915.

Like many orthodox Christians, Nelly was led to believe that mediumship was demonic in nature, but as she opened her mind to learn more about it she recognized that the basic teachings of Jesus – Love thy neighbor..., Do unto others..., and You reap what you sow – are also the teachings emerging from the credible mediums of the day, and that mediumship could take her beyond the blind faith of orthodox religion to true faith, or conviction. She soon recognized that mediumship is the foundation of the Bible and that the clergy was misinterpreting passages in the Old Testament in condemning it. She was influenced by Sir Oliver

Lodge's 1909 book, "The Survival of Man" and "The Drama of Love and Death," by Edward Carpenter. "Throughout the whole of my study of this subject," she wrote, "the fact that has impressed me most forcibly is the cheap, indifferent, irreverent way in which mankind receives and treats the revelation God so graciously makes to us of what lies beyond the grave. Mankind in general, and as a whole, does not want to know that there is another world besides this one, much less any details about it"

Nelly's search for evidence that Rolf had survived his physical death began with two visits with medium Alfred Vout Peters, the same medium Sir Oliver Lodge saw soon after the death of his son, Raymond (See Chapter One). Rolf communicated and gave his mother much evidential information, including the names of relatives, a description of the interior of her home, the names of two of her servants, and the fact that she had problems cultivating strawberries in her garden because of birds.

After the two sittings with Peters, Nelly sat with Mrs. Brittain and received even more evidential communication, including the names of three uncles, John, Frank, and "Major," the latter a nickname accurately communicated, while also referring to his brother as "the kid," just as he had when alive.

Through the mediumship of Mrs. Wesley Adams, Rolf told his mother of his joy at finding he was still himself and that he had misjudged the nature of the afterlife when still in the flesh. He further told his mother that her prayers had expedited his progress on that side.

He said that his mother's brother and sister, who had both passed over as babies, were now grown and were there to meet him when he arrived on the other side, and that the sister, Annie, had escorted him to the third plane and was now serving as one of his guides. The sittings with Gladys Osborne Leonard, which make up most of her book, began some three years after Rolf's transition. Apparently, during that time, Rolf befriended Claude, the subject of Chapter Three.

Reader Alert: As with Chapter One, the communication coming through Feda, Mrs. Leonard's spirit control, varies. At times, Feda will say, "Rolf says..." or "He says..." and at other times she relays Rolf's words in the first person, e.g., "Mother, I was with you last night when..." But now and then, Feda will express her own thoughts or question Rolf if she does not understand what he is trying to communicate. Occasionally, she switches abruptly from the third person to the first person or from stating something about Rolf to Rolf explaining it in his own words. And she sometimes refers to herself in the third person, e.g., "Feda thinks this *is what Rolf is trying to say..." As with Sir Oliver Lodge in Chapter One and Mrs. L. Kelway-Bamber in Chapter Three, Nelly Little corrects and smoothes out the sometimes faulty grammar of Feda. The words below in standard print come directly from the book, while those in italics are those of the editor of this book.*

On April 18, 1918, the communication began with Feda stating that Rolf was there and that he was sitting on the corner of his mother's bed the prior night. Nelly responded that she could not hear him. Feda replied:

✳✳✳

They were too excited to do much. Claude and he had been talking together, and found they liked many of the same things, and were much alike in disposition. It is a coincidence that those who meet on the other side often seem to have had the same sort of spiritual experience whilst on the earth plane. Claude and Rolf both have a faculty of expressing themselves and telling about their real life over there – whilst many boys over there who go through some of the same experiences could not possibly express them through Feda. Words go from them and they can't get them through...

When first Rolf began to go on long journeys, he had guides with him, in case he should forget to concentrate and come to a standstill, as in driving a car...The first few weeks Rolf puttered around a lot, surveying the country, and he thought the scenery he was in was very much like what he had been used to, and he said to himself, "This bit I am in is very much like England at home," and then he went to France and he thought France in the spirit realm seemed just about the same distance as France is from England on the earth plane. So he went to one of the guides, who help the new spirits and show them how to travel, just like a Cook's tourist guide on the earth plane, and he asked him about it. This guide showed Rolf a map of the spirit world, and the position of England in the spirit world is exactly relative and just over England on the earth plane, and so on with France and all the other countries; they are just over each other on this map. He could see around the earth plane, first the astral, then the second sphere, and then his own third sphere, right on through the fourth, fifth, sixth, and seventh spheres, and round about the seventh sphere the Infinite force...and swimming about in this Infinite force are all the other planets, which are worlds but which looked like little ships on this map. It was a very wonderful map, not like a piece of paper, but really a model of the universe, and Rolf could see that some of the other planets are much bigger than our own. These planets are all inhabited, Rolf was told, but by different forms of life than ours...On the better known planets, the people are shaped like those on our planet, only they are generally smaller ...Finally, the earth plane, Rolf was told, will crumble to pieces, but it won't do that until people have got so God-like that they can do without it as a school, for the earth plane is simply God's school, where people are put in a difficult human body, to promote and purify character.

Nelly asked if Jesus did not atone for all. Speaking for Rolf, Feda responded that Jesus was an example, but people didn't follow his example. Rolf said that the Bible had become so misinterpreted that people were confused as to the messages. Asked about the devil, Rolf said that the devil is in oneself, that it is "earth-earthy," not a creation of God.

Just as the beautiful forceful Spirit of God permeates the spirit plane, so when you do a wrong, thing, and try to persuade yourself it is right, you are pandering to the devil in you. Every man is born with an ability to distinguish the difference between the God in him and the flesh. When a new soul comes into a little baby's body, the soul part is always much greater than the evil part. As a child grows, the reason begins to grow, and it begins to have the ability of showing which it will choose, the earth side or the God inside. Pandering to the flesh means absorbing more of the devil into itself, and if it passes over without atoning for that – atoning not in words but in deeds – if a man does an evil deed, he must do a good one after it to balance. The Roman Catholic religion has got a germ of truth in it, though it is very much abused – a man must do penance; he either has got to do good, or he can't go the same place.

This is the real secret of the thing. We must go through prayer and meditation alone, by ourselves, and consult the God within. The God within can be always got at, if we only look for It, putting self and selfish desire on one side. The God within is more easily got at by prayer and meditation than by any other means.

A little thing which we call Conscience, but which is really the Voice of God, will say to us: "Well, I know it is not right to do that," but our weaker self replies, "I want to do it so much, I will pretend it is right." It is more difficult for the God within to get through the flesh, because the flesh is more apparent to us. It is easier for the God within to get through it if we put ourselves in an attitude of prayer. It allies us to the Divine by lifting up the soul and mind above morbid desires. When you are in that attitude, earthly things seem small by the side of spiritual things. You really switch on to the Divine, and there things appear as they really are.

But when people wish to do sordid things, and wrong – they don't do this; they hoodwink themselves purposely...

Mother, you may think I am moralising, but how wonderful it is. I can never tell you until you come over here yourself. I have to say my words to Feda, and she has to push them into the medium's brain, and open her mouth to say them out to you.

When you come over, you'll want your clothes, at first, anyhow. You wouldn't want to go about in short white skirts and bare feet. Why, when people came to call, you would run away and hide yourself.

[Nelly asked if people actually came to call there.] Yes, but only the people you like come, as like attracts like, and the people you do not like keep away.

Rolf said that he sees a great deal of his grandfather (Nelly's father) and that they had become great pals and would often talk about Nelly. At a sitting on July 9, 1918, Rolf said that he had had a lot of experiences since he last talked with his mother. He told her that he had been learning control, not psychic control, but the control of spiritual, mental, and physical forces.

You know these forces are everywhere – the physical, of course, on the physical plane, the mental belongs to the physical plane, too – it develops on the physical plane.

When a soul goes into a little baby's body, there is no mentality there – just as an idiot may have a brain but no mentality. The mentality has to be developed on the physical plane. Some people would disagree with that – some think that the soul belongs to the brain. The soul belongs to the life force., but it does not bring it like a "bump" of anything. I then contend, as the guides showed me, that the mental is developed on the physical plane according to how the spiritual is able to manifest through the physical.

Now on the spirit sphere, there is no Physical, but there is the Mental and the Spiritual – the Mentality, the Individuality, and the Personality, which is brought into being in the earth body. That is connected then with the spirit body, and the spirit body, being of a higher degree than the earth body, the Mental is more easily able to function in it.

Now what I was learning on the sixth sphere was all about this – how it got there, what degree and quality it has, and most important of all, how to use it wisely and well.

[Feda speaking independent of Rolf] He remembers everything he told you when you were here last. Feda forgets, because she sees so many people, but Rolf remembers everything he told you. His memory is wonderful now. He says, "I've only got to be told a fact in the spirit sphere, and it remains always in my consciousness...

The physical was shown to him, both by instruments and pictures, to be a gross chord, and a heavy major chord. The mental was shown to be a degree lighter. Like the sub-dominant of the major chord is the mental and the spiritual, whilst in the body is the minor. He'll tell you why presently. It's the minor whilst the spirit is imprisoned in the flesh, because it's what you might call "the hidden Life veiled by the Body."

Take the average crowd – 80 people out of 100 will be purely physical – 10 percent only would be spiritual in any way – the spiritual is always a little in the background. It must necessarily be so – you must wash your body, you must feed your body, you must care for your body – the body is the fore-ground whilst you live in the body. God meant it to be so, but when you get out of the body the spiritual is going to be major and minor as well...

You must bring the spiritual from behind – the minor, into the foreground and let people see it. Rolf says, "It gives them something to hang on to...One day the spiritual will express itself in a spirit body and become major..."

We were told that it is far more possible to bring the spiritual through into the physical than people have wished to do so far, and we were shown how – that there were always hands of guides ready to give instructions to those who need it. What pleased me even more than the knowledge of the guides and helpers was to be told that every person had it within themselves to go within and draw on the spiritual power, and bring it through the mental, and into the physical, so that they would realise how beautiful the spiritual was, how true, how glorious, so that the spiritual would shine through them in good works, in good actions.

The guide took Rolf to see a case in which a person would go into the spiritual but not bring it back with him. It involved a clergyman who prayed regularly and was able to raise himself into a state of spiritual ecstasy. However, when he got up from his knees, he became fussy and fault-finding, often grumbling to his wife and bullying the household help. Rolf was shown another man – one who rarely went to his knees but who loved his fellow man and served them with what little he had.

Protestations and prayers are of little avail if one's works do not show the true light within. The body is like a window, the soul is like a light. How can you help anyone by drawing down the blind? The blind must be up and the light must shine through. If it is hidden, what is the use of it? I am speaking now of the highway of light. Each one of you on the earth plane who can show a light brightly through your window is helping to guide some weary traveler – but you give little help to others if you hide the light, or if for some reason or other it cannot be seen...What an awful highway it would be if there were no light at all! What a dreary path!

Rolf went on to say that he was shown the life of Henry VIII, a man who believed himself religious through self-deception – a failure to exercise his mentality and think correctly through his brain. When his physical senses wanted to do something not spiritual, he tried to do it before his higher self, his conscience, could prevent it. Like most people who do wrong, he chose not to think, because he knew that if he did think, his body would be deprived of some pleasure. Rolf went on to talk about the Bible.

Even ordinary history, so to speak, of even a few hundred years ago has been so distorted and so misquoted that people say, "What can you expect of nineteen-hundred years ago?" The thing is, as you were saying before the sitting, the Old Testament is not to be taken too literally, but must be taken in the symbolic sense. If you went by the dates as given in the authorized version, Adam and Eve were said to be created long after mankind had existed on this earth. You must not take time as it is given in this sense – it's taken too literally and that's wrong. Even a report of an ordinary lecture doesn't get given perfectly. There is nothing perfect on this earth plane, because man has distorted it. It was perfect when God gave it, but man has distorted it.

We here speak of things plainly, because they are real things, and everything that God gave us is clean, if we think of it cleanly.

Certain parts of the Bible were not written by really good people – but put in by scribes afterwards. Some parts of the Bible should be censored – you know what I mean. God only speaks of beautiful, and good, and wise things. He does not speak of filth, and man has used this to disprove all that is wise and true and beautiful in the Bible.

Of course, sacrifice should not be necessary – but if it is necessary, what a good thing we can make it...

Since I have passed over, and you began to understand, there have been in the months since it was brought home to you, thousands and thousands who have passed over. Out of every thousand mourners, five-hundred are realising the same thing. I do not know that they realise it quite the same as you do, but the germ of it is there, and is only waiting for that big move in which a spring will be touched, and these people will find their own thoughts materialised in the thoughts of other people. They are all going to come out, too, and be banded together...

It is all in the process of development, but you'll be surprised to know that in every village, in every little hamlet, there are spiritualists. The tragic part about it, and the part you've got to help them in, is that they're all afraid of being laughed at. People are very much like sheep. If there is a leader and it is to their advantage to follow, they'll follow him, but they do not know yet what there is to follow.

Feda had a difficult time getting the name "Leslie" through Mrs. Leonard's brain, but finally got Nelly to understand that she was referring to the son of a man in her church, a young soldier who had died fourteen days earlier. She said that Rolf, who knew Leslie before the war, was helping him adjust to his new environment, and had brought Leslie to the sitting that day. Feda said Rolf wanted to talk about mental power and how things on the earth plane can be materialised – actually brought into the material world by mental force properly directed.

Now, darling, I told you at a previous sitting how the things on the earthly plane were helped to grow, and the places were helped in the building by mental effort – concentrated – but there had to be some material, some foundation for that mental effort to work upon.

I think I told you – correct me if I did not – that the houses were built one-hundred times more quickly in the spirit world than on the earth plane, because the minds of all those engaged in building were conscious of exactly what had to be done. They were all concentrated on the work in hand. Now they do this because they are taught soon after they come over, that that is the way to build a place quickly and well, or to do anything quickly and well. You see, mother, on the earth plane, people are not taught concentration, not in a definite way.

Thought, to be creative on the earth plane, has to be very strong in one individual, and you will notice that when an individual does create anything to a very remarkable degree, such as wonderful paintings, extraordinary compositions, clever books, that person is very one-sided as a rule. Most so-called geniuses are one-sided, because they have thrown all their mental energies, and consequently their physical energies, too, into one channel. Now, this is the important point – thought, which is not wrong in any one individual, is not creative unless you gather a collection of individuals together in one room, or one building, and focus their attention on one thing. For example, an audience watching a play or hearing a speaker or preacher. There you get collective thought, which may not contain one individual's strong thought, but, anyhow, collective thought of some kind or another all focused in one direction. Now, that may not be creative of anything tangible, but that it is a force is proved by its effect on the action of the performer, who feeling the concentration upon him, will feel called upon or helped to do his utmost. Also, that collective thought sways the audience itself...

What I am interested in is that this great collective thought is creative of evil – not evil in the sense it was sent out to accomplish, but other evils. You know the saying, "Curses come home to roost." Well, this collective destructive thought "comes home to roost," but it comes home under a different disguise; that is why after any unreal war there is always a plague.

You see, mother, it is like this, It's like a great force projected to another great force, and both sides are thinking the same thing. When that great collective thought meets the other great collective thought from the other side, they merge into each other, and actually give birth to a second, or rather to a third evil...

Now, just as that collective thought can breed evil, just so collective thought, with construction in the object instead of destruction, could bring forth a most beautiful peace and happiness in the world. This is being learnt slowly on the earth plane. If only ten people in one town think that way, they will affect others in a little while, and the spreading of good is very rapid; so never lose heart when you see so much evil and trouble around you. Think rightly, and send out progressive and helpful thoughts.

At a sitting on November 12, 1918 at 7 p.m., the day the Armistice was signed, Rolf began with a "Hip! Hip! Hooray!" and told his mother that the great force that had been hurling itself toward destruction had been removed. However, he said that there would continue to be a great deal of destructive and resentful thought coming from Germany for some time to come. He proceeded to talk about the spirit body.

When the spirit comes over here at the death of the body, it occupies a spirit body, but it is possible for the spirit to leave the physical whilst the physical body is still alive, and to enter a body which is called the astral body. That astral body looks very like the spirit body, but it is of slightly coarser material. It is made of a certain amount of matter – that is, matter which is tangible, and which would be pronounced as matter by anyone in the astral, but would be called intangible by anyone in your world.

Your body is intangible to us to a great extent. Some of us learnt to perceive it. I have learnt to do so, but not all of us do.

Now, darling, you know when you want to see us what difficulties there are in the way of your doing so. We have almost the same difficulty in seeing you, only it is rather easier for us than it is for you. The reason you cannot see us is that we are of a different degree, or kind of matter, and we are operating in a different dimension to you.

[Nelly asked him to explain what he meant by dimension.] It is a state or condition of being, technically called a dimension. Now, when you develop for clairvoyance, you have to attune yourself to our condition mentally. Now, you can only do this for a very short while at a time. That's why visions come and go so quickly.

You could not exist at that rate of vibration – which is very much higher than yours – for long at a time, the strain would be too great. But when we want to get into your conditions, our difficulty is not so great as yours is when you try to see us, because you are at a lower rate of vibration, and it is easier to accustom oneself to a lower rate, or a slower pace, for a time than it is to a higher one...

You only see by vibration, for just as the drum of the ear is attuned to catch the vibration of sound, so the retina of the eyes is attuned to catch the vibration of visibility.

Now, everything on the earth plane goes at a certain rate of vibration, a little more or a little less, but the further you get from the earth plane, the more rapid becomes the rate of vibration. By the time you get really to the spirit world, say to the third sphere, the rate is too rapid for us to be easily perceived by anyone on the earth plane. A proof of this assertion is that all so-called "hauntings," "ghosts," etc. are people from the astral – murderers, suicides, unhappy earth-bound spirits. The bright, happy, beautiful spirits are not often seen to return to earth; they are living at too high a rate of vibration to be easily visible.

Rolf likened the earth plane to a motor vehicle designed to go 40 miles per hour and his plane to one designed to go 100 miles per hour, explaining that the faster vehicle can much more easily adjust to going 40 mph, than the slower vehicle can to going 100 mph. Thus, he could hear his mother much more easily than she could hear him. He then discussed clairvoyance.

To be clairvoyant, one would have to put oneself into a certain mental state, shutting off for the time being all evidence of physical surroundings. This is the usual way. There are rare occasions where people are clairvoyant while they are doing some quiet earthly task. That is not what we would call naturally clairvoyance or a developed clairvoyance. The better the mental attitude on the earth plane, the easier conditions will it give for intercourse between the two worlds. But the majority of people have all their thoughts concentrated on material things alone. It is like shutting the gate or door in our faces, and we can knock on the door and knock on the door, but they've bolted and barred it.

But, if the majority, even only a small majority, would think about us and try to acknowledge our existence, or even to wish to acknowledge it, and if they would endeavour to conduct their earth lives in such a manner as to feel they were fitting themselves for a life to come, they would be making the way clear for us – throwing the door open, and the intercourse which would follow would be of a beautiful, mutual, and helpful kind...

The Spirit of Christ, through Jesus, opened the door then, and let the spiritual light flood over the world. But people didn't really follow the teaching that came through that open door, and only intermittently, since then, has that door opened a little, and then closed again.

Now, mother, the war came and thousands and thousands of us flew through that door into the other world, and so great was the force of loving thought and longing which followed us, that it prompted the door open, making it kind of a wedge. The loving thoughts, diverted from earthly gains, sent in waves of anxious love to follow us wherever we went. Few of them knew where we'd gone, but they sent out the thought to wherever we were, so, naturally, those thoughts all came the same way.

Now, the wedge is there, the door is propped open. I do hope and pray they will not withdraw that wedge by forgetting to follow us in thought, and not wanting to know where we are gone.

At a sitting on February 9, 1919, Rolf told his mother that man is always creating physical conditions, and God is always trying to pour over them, and into them a spiritual essence.

Sometimes man creates physical conditions of such an evil and destructive nature that God's share is unable to operate directly through the man-made conditions. But, when God sees these conditions having a wrong and bad result and influence, He brings the spiritual part to bear on those evil results, to ameliorate the results to innocent persons thereby bringing into effect something which is often spoken of as the law of compensation.

You may have noticed that the innocent seem to suffer from the evil-doing of others. Yes, that is so, and until man realises the far-reaching and terrible effects for evil-doing, by seeing it visited on the innocent, a better state or condition of things will not be possible. In other words, the innocent often have to suffer because of the guilty, as an example, and also as an appeal to those who love justice and to whose hands have the power of remedying the bad and evil social conditions which make the injustice possible. to take up the work of reaching truth – the truth about cause and effect – so that man will gradually, even quickly, I think, come to realise the effort which is directed to pure material gain, and that only in working for the good of the community, and the uplifting of humanity, putting self on one side, can any lasting good be gained by the individual.

It's a puzzle, Feda says. Does it make sense, because I lose it, waiting for the next words?

I'm just saying that to make it clear that God is always, so to speak, in a kind of partnership with man, just as I told you before, good is always attendant on evil waiting for a chance to counteract it, just as day waits upon night.

The worst of it is that man won't let God's part in things be apparent. He does such evil and selfish things, that it is like pushing the power of good on one side in order to accomplish evil and exercise the power of evil...

I do not believe that evil is ever perpetuated by someone with the willful knowledge that it is evil. No, it is committed through the lack of true knowledge and insight, which, if possessed, even to a minor degree, would prevent anyone from committing wicked or cruel actions wantonly.

Now, you see God's share in the war was the giving again of His Spirit through Christ, in order that we might be helped and uplifted in the hours of trial.

On June 16, 1919, at 11 a.m., Nelly Little sat with Mary Harris, a direct-voice medium. Also present were Eliza Kelway-Bamber, the mother of Claude (See Chapter Three) and the Rev. C. Drayton Thomas (See Introduction). The direct-voice form of mediumship is not the same as the trance-voice of Mrs. Leonard. In the direct-voice the communicating spirit does not use the medium's vocal cords. Rather, the voice comes through independently of the medium's body, seemingly emanating from above or to the side of the medium and usually amplified by a "trumpet" held by spirit hands while floating around the room. It is said that spirits materialize the necessary vocal organs by using the ectoplasm coming from the medium and others.

At 8 p.m. that same day, Nelly Little sat with Mrs. Leonard. Rolf, who had communicated earlier at the Harris sitting, explained the modus operandi of the direct-voice to his mother. As Feda communicated her own words, not just those of Rolf, the distinction is made in the transcript of the sitting.

Feda: Hee! Hee! Hee! I was there this morning at the voice sitting. I didn't squeak when I spoke. Rolf says I did squeak – that I spoke in a more squeaky voice than usual. Claude says I squeaked, too, but I didn't.

Nelly: Yes, we heard you, Feda. We heard Harmony say, "Feda is here," then you were away quickly [Harmony was Mrs. Harris's spirit control.]

Feda: That wasn't Harmony that spoke; that was Feda's own self that said, "Feda is here." Did you notice that when Rolf spoke, he spoke a little below you? He tried to get higher, and then he got a little above you. He didn't seem as if he could get quite on the level with you.

Rolf: There were a lot of very good spirits there. They came just because we were there – people who had written books. Mr. Stead was there and Mr. Drayton's father and grandfather were there, too.

Feda: Rolf says, "Did I know that my father was there, too? He was so interested, and he said, 'My word, if only I had known this when I was here (there?). How interested I would have been.'"

Rolf: Now, I told you mother, that I'd been studying about it beforehand. It does help, because many people who have been dozens of times to voice mediums have not been able to get through, like we did. Claude did pretty well, but he'd been studying it, too...

I could see very plainly that the power was not only taken from the medium, but was in and taken from you, the sitters. Now you remember that ether that I was telling you about – if you get a concentrated or stronger form of ether, we call it etheric force or etheric matter. Now you've got a certain quantity of this in your physical body – everybody has, but some have more than others. It isn't only that some have more than others, but some are able to give it out more, or perhaps it would be better still to say it can be drawn from them more than it can from others. [Apparently speaking of what is otherwise called "ectoplasm."]

Feda: Rolf noticed that a great deal of power came from you, and came from Claude's mother, too – in fact, you both gave out an equal quantity, and as you were sitting opposite each other, it balanced things very nicely. He noticed there was a gap in the power where there shouldn't have been [Nelly noted that there was a big table between the medium and Claude's mother]. That shouldn't have been; another sitter would have been better there.

Rolf: Now, that medium had tremendous power, and her etheric force was wonderful, and not only had she got a lot of force but, unlike some mediums, she gave a tremendous lot out – so much so that I was afraid she would be internally exhausted.

After you'd been sitting about two or three minutes, I began to see quite a ring of what looked to me first of all like mist, but it was really the power beginning to circulate, and you noticed that she tried to place you negative and positive.

Feda: Your mother wouldn't know that, Rolf.

Rolf: She wouldn't let you sit just where you thought – she was trying to find negative and positive. A woman is generally considered negative and a man is positive, but of course there are exceptions to that rule, because if you see a la-di-da sort of fellow, very effeminate, he's negative, even though he's a man, and you get a very aggressive woman, masculine type, she's positive, but they, of course, are exceptions. Now, of course, there are some lucky people, but few and far between, who can be negative or positive according to circumstances or conditions. You're like that, and Claude's mother is like that.

Mr. Draytie (C. Drayton Thomas) is positive, as he ought to be, but you and Claude's mother belong to the fortunate class who can be either. It requires great self-control to be like that, and I've noticed, mother, that you've got that, because you often make yourself patient in order to get a little further into a matter. You are very philosophical – you always accustom yourself to a condition if you can – you don't waste time in useless repining, neither does Claude's mother, so you see you were two very good points, and Mr. Draytie, being just in the right place, formed a good point, too, so quite a lot of power flowed around.

Now, I saw this etheric force joining itself up with the medium, and connecting with her reservoir of power, which was enormous in itself. So great was the accumulation that she seemed almost wrapped in this power, and I saw her guides. She had several guides there –not only Harmony – because I saw two gentlemen there.

There was another rather young lady there, but older than Harmony. She belonged to the medium, and they began to draw the force, and it seemed to come right through her solar plexus, and up through her chest and throat, and partly out of her mouth, so it looked to me like a thick white stream issuing from her mouth.

I put my hand close to it – not intentionally – it felt like a strong stream or current of electricity. I noticed that the guides waited until it was flowing outwards, and I could see how dangerous it would have been if anyone had gripped, or touched even, any article that that force was connected with, as you would have checked that which was her very life force contained in this stream of power.

She, the medium, was supplying twenty times what you were supplying. This stream of power was playing on to the trumpet, and then I saw that the guides were manipulating the power into the trumpet, first of all to raise it from the floor, and then to materialize the voices inside it.

You know the way you use a garden hose? Well, the power was being used like you would use a garden hose. You could direct it on to a sheet that was hung up. I saw that the voice was materialized inside the trumpet, but I could see also that it was possible, when the power got to this stage, to speak without using the trumpet.

At one time there were really two voices speaking at once. Can you remember this?

I think that one voice was really outside to begin with, and then took the trumpet afterwards. You noticed that one voice started before the other finished, didn't you?

Did you notice how at the end of a sentence I'd lose mine a bit? Well, I'd get so much etheric force into the trumpet, and when I'd used that up I had to fall back, as it were, and draw some more power in quickly, and then you remember I started again a little more strongly, and of course don't forget that one spirit will spin the power out better than another spirit will.

I think the more practice one had, the more one would be able to draw the power in for the next sentence whilst speaking the one.

Nelly: Just like a singer learning to take breath and to control her breathing power?

Rolf: Mum, you are clever. You always know just what I am wanting to say. Yes, that etheric force we draw from the medium is like breath to us – we have to learn how to control it. Now next time, mum, I think I shall be able to do far better. You know, I had two goes at it... I never went away for a minute. I was most interested. Whether we were speaking, or whether we were doing stunts with the musical box – it would have been very dangerous to the medium if anyone had interfered with that musical box. I felt she was in a very peculiar position all the time. There was pressure on the veins and arteries, and if anything had happened to increase suddenly the pressure, she might have had a hemorrhage.

Nelly asked for a better explanation of Mrs. Leonard's trance-voice mediumship and how Rolf was managing to communicate. Although Feda struggled at times with some of the words used by Rolf, she managed to get nearly all of his explanations through.

You know, mum, I'm giving my own original ideas, my own version of it as a typewriter. It is like a telephone, but to me a typewriter is the better simile. If it's a trance medium, the control is the operator, or typist, as you call it. The communicator, such as myself, would then be in the position of the dictator. Can you see the idea, mum? Now, as we are communicating through this class of medium, we'd better take this kind of mediumship first. Now, the brain of the medium is like the keyboard. I know that I'm right...We know that people's brains differ in capacity in power. I say that the more developed a medium's brain is, the larger the keyboard is at the service of the control and communicator.

Now, you'll ask, "In what way is the brain like a keyboard for the control?" It's different in this way. Instead of representing separate letters, it represents words – whole words – ideas – different emotions – in fact, you can run the whole gamut of human experience and sensation upon it...Here we have the medium's brain and we have the control hovering over the medium, the communicating spirit adjacent. Now, the control knows that there is a spirit there, wishing to send messages through her. She thereupon brings her power to take control over the medium's consciousness – the medium having prepared herself by becoming as passive as possible.

Now, it may take the control five minutes, it may take twenty minutes, but what happens is that the control's spirit is temporarily drawn into the physical organism of the medium, while the medium's spirit is temporarily ejected...The spirit of the medium is still connected with her body by the vital cord. Her spirit may travel and have some wonderful experiences of its own on the spirit planes, or it may hover two or three yards away from her body. This medium's spirit, I have noticed, is usually close, about two or three yards roughly...It looks very much like her own body, only not so solid, because it is still connected by the vital cord, and a certain amount of the power is running away from the spirit through the cord into the body. If the spirit were disconnected by death, it would become more solid, that is, more tangible, because it would not need to put the life force into the body but would keep it with itself.

I notice that the spirit body of the medium appears to be clothed in a somewhat intangible duplicate. If you understand, it's more an astral shape. The clothes are more an astral shape caused by the close connection between the spirit and the physical body – in other words, it's like a thought clothing wrought automatically round the spirit. It appears to rest in the air in a horizontal position, as if it were sleeping, but I also know that it is possible for the spirit to travel, as I said before...

Directly, the spirit oozes out of the medium's body, the control's spirit is drawn in. By being drawn in, I do not mean that all the spirit body of the control is drawn in contained within the stomach and chest of the medium, because that is where it would have to be, but it may be partly outside her form, looking like an outer covering or husk. But as spirit can penetrate though matter, part of the spirit may penetrate the actual flesh, and by this contact, the mind of the controlling spirit may become aware of any physical disturbance in the body of the medium. – and it is a very good thing that it is so sometimes, because it helps the control to receive impressions from the communicating spirit, and it helps the communicating spirit to register such useful evidence as the manner of his passing over, or anything that might have happened to him in the physical life which would be a good test of identity. For instance, if a spirit had once broken his arm, we might want to give that as evidence, and if he were clever enough to do so, the communicating spirit would think of it strongly enough to give the impression of the broken arm in the arm of the medium...We find it much easier to give the feeling of it first to the medium's body, because directly the control feels that; she understands that it is something sent by the communicating spirit, and that can be done in one second.

The nerve thrill is sent at once to give the pain. This is felt at once by the control, whereas you know the difficulty there often is in getting through some specified word. This is very important. I should think of arm, broken arm. Now the control would hear me say, "broken arm," but the difficulty is that the control, by being in the body of the medium, is to a certain extent limited, because she is in a condition which is not her own natural one. She certainly does not hear

118

what the communicating spirit says as clearly as if she were outside the medium's organism. But we'll say, for the sake of argument, that she has heard me say, "I once broke my arm." Her task is now to say that through the [medium's] body.

You know, in fact everyone knows, that you cannot speak one syllable without using the brain in some way. I don't know much about the brain, in a technical sense, but I know that if the medium's mouth, or anyone else's mouth, is opened, if only to say "Bah, bah," some part of the brain must have been used...

The control, therefore, has the task of manipulating the brain, which is the keyboard, to make the medium say, "I once broke my arm." The reason I liken it to a keyboard is because the control has to look for a particular key, or sign corresponding the most nearly to the words she wishes the medium to say.

Now, it may be that the medium's vocabulary does not contain certain words and expressions that the spirit would use, or it may be that the medium would be in the habit of expressing herself quite differently – do you see?

So that if the medium would not use those words – "I once broke my arm," for example, the control would have to find the nearest expression to it, and at the same time, would find some word suggesting "broken," and would perhaps not get the idea of "arm" at all at first, but merely "limb," possibly getting "arm" a little later.

It is a strange thing that the nearer the first word found on the keyboard to the desired one, the more quickly will the desired one be found. For instance, the control might get "shoulder" or "hand" – that would quickly suggest "arm," because the control is, so to speak, feeling her way step by step...

Now, the more used a control becomes to a particular medium's organism, the more proficient will she become in quickly and correctly finding the desire word on the keyboard – just as an expert typist quickly finds the signs and letters on the typewriter, whilst an inexperienced operator is floundering about.

Well, darling, it isn't so much that we look for it, as that we feel for it. Can you imagine typewriting in the dark? An expert typist could type even in the dark.

Rolf went on to explain that a control can work well with one medium, but may experience much difficulty working with another medium. Feda agreed and said she couldn't get through Mary Harris at all, after which Rolf said that Mrs. Harris's guides were unable to use Mrs. Leonard's power. Rolf continued:

Now, when a control has had a certain amount of experience in giving sittings through one medium, she will then venture to try to develop her sense of hearing more acutely through that medium, knowing that if she cannot hear the particular word, she can give up the attempt and fall back on her old custom of feeling a suitable expression or word. Whilst she is learning to hear better, a slight delay or difficulty may be apparent to the sitter, which, of course, would be occasioned by the control trying a different method.

You notice that sometimes Feda is very successful in spelling specified words or names, by drawing them letter by letter in the air. – that is, tracing them with the medium's finger. That is a third method, but Feda told me that she had been controlling her medium three or four years before she was able to attempt this third method.

Now, Feda very often hears the word or name from the communicating spirit, but only when she is not striving unnaturally for it. The difficulty is so much less apparent when I come prepared with certain things to say, which I can pour through in a quiet and steady stream, than if you suddenly held me up and said, "Do you remember your mother's name?"

Of course, I remember it, but directly you ask for the special word, which, mind, must be one word, and no other out of the thousands it might be, you make the control anxious, and a kind of strained effect occurs in the medium's brain.

Now, you know that in normal life people do not achieve things so well, or so easily, when they are striving and anxious, and it is just the same directly the control becomes anxious. She closes at once those more subtle and delicate means of direct hearing from the communicating spirit, and falls back on the more elementary method again. Even that is cramped and limited, strained, in fact, by the sense of striving after one particular thing. The control then would possibly get a name, or perhaps an initial, which would be the same, or very like the one required. Do you remember, Feda apparently was not sure if my brother's name was Alan or Alec, but she kept getting Ala, Ala in the first sitting you had with her.

You see what I mean – the control would be lucky if she found the right name, if you were pushing her and straining her. It seems to me that the power produces better results when it's all poured through from our side, not being continually stopped and dammed...

I think I said before that we might speak to the control in two ways – one, by thought or telepathy; two, by actual words; but in many cases, communication is given much more quickly by thought. For instance, if I were describing a house with a certain room in it, how much more quickly and thoroughly could I give it to the control in a series of quick pictures than by saying word for word what the house looked like, and the details of the rooms, because, as I told you the other day, the control may not be able to hear my spirit voice clearly, whilst she is in the physical body...

You might ask me, how I show the control these pictures, as I call them, and what is the difficulty of showing them? Why does she get them wrong as so often happens? Now, you know that if you in the physical body have some particular object presented to your sight, the impression of that thing has to be photographed on your brain before you will be conscious what it is you are looking at. Your eyes may be looking at a thing, but unless your brain takes up the consciousness of it, you don't see it, proving that one must become conscious of everything in one's brain before one perceives it through sight, or touch, or any other sense...

Now, the control's difficulty is the same. She has to use the brain of the medium to perceive the pictures that I show, and if the brain of the mediums does not become conscious of them, the control herself does not know, do you see, because the control is not looking at me through the medium's eyes, or through her own eyes, but with consciousness first. So you see the reason why it is easier to give an impression or mental picture of a certain place is because one can suggest it, if you understand, to the mind of the medium, and then the control becomes conscious of it.

Of course, when a spirit and a control, and a sitter have worked together as often as we three have, and are so much in harmony and sympathy, it becomes much easier. It is just like working in an office that you are used to and with people that you're used to, and like, or with a typewriter, or with any instrument you are familiar with.

Other observations, thoughts, ideas, and teachings expressed by Rolf include:

Spirit Separation: In the majority of cases, the spirit would take about three days to collect itself entirely, and separate itself entirely from the body, but after that it would take a week or two weeks, or even three weeks, before it could manifest to anyone upon the earth plane again. Jesus had developed and realised so many divine gifts while in the body that He found it quite easy to exercise His power immediately on shaking Himself free from the physical. The better you are in your earth life, spiritually and morally, the more easily you will be able to exercise your consciousness on entering the spirit life. Two or three days is about the time it takes a spirit to leave the body, unless there is some condition present which forces the spirit out into an absolutely separate existence, such as fire, or drowning, in which case the spirit is carefully nursed and induced to sleep for some time in the spirit world.

Third Plane Link: Everyone on the third plane is still in touch with, and waiting for, someone they love – which makes the link with the old habits and likes. Till you and father come over I am glad I can stay here, but, of course, one is more personal and individual on the third sphere than on the seventh sphere. Now, we'll say that you both come over, and that you live with me on the third sphere, working for a good many years, until, in fact, everyone whom we are interested in or fond of, in a personal sense, has joined us. When they have, we should instinctively want to progress upwards – to go onwards and upwards – and we should go on to the fourth, or possibly the fifth sphere. It should not be new to us, because long before we should go to live there, we should have been visiting there and learning all about the different conditions, and we might live for even centuries on these spheres before we should be ready to go to the sixth.

Advancing to Higher Spheres: Before one can be sufficiently advanced to live on the higher spheres, one has to be able to concentrate at will, on anything, at any time. There is a great reason for this. The conditions of life on the higher spheres are more dependent on the mental power than those of the third sphere. For instance, I told you I have a body, which apparently is a duplicate of the one I had on the earth plane – that is, I have lungs which I can expand and fill in with air; I have a heart, which seems to beat and pulsate; I have liver, kidney, and other internal organs, but they are not used in the same way as on the earth plane because I do not eat the same coarse food, which requires to go through the liver, kidneys, etc. I, in a way, absorb food, or fuel for my body through the pores of my skin, as well as through the air that I breathe; but as one goes higher one has less of the material in the composition of one's spirit body, though the outer appearance is the same – in fact, the bodies of those on the higher spheres have a lesser proportion of actual atoms of matter in their composition than I have. Therefore, these atoms are more tightly held together – the atmosphere is lighter there – all the conditions are different – everything, or nearly everything is done by concentration of mind and wise direction of power and force on these higher planes.

Individuality: I wish to state emphatically – first, that we do not lose one iota of individuality gained through our experience on earth and the lower planes. What we do lose is selfish desires. We lose that wish to strive for self only, and that fact sometimes gets confounded in people's minds on the lower spheres. and even more so when they endeavor to transmit it through the brain to some writer, philosopher, medium, or anyone they try to work through, and then one gets the false impression that the sinking of selfish desires means the losing of personality. Never shall we lose our individuality, only the selfish impression of it.

Remembering After Death: Mother, [what I am telling you about afterlife conditions] is never forgotten. You forget it consciously, but you remember it subconsciously, and when you are brought into the conditions requiring that knowledge, you tap the subconscious and up comes everything you have learned about it. I know from people who have come over here and have heard about our spirit life, and even thought it was "tommy-rot," in fact, discarded it altogether, but when they came face to face with it, it all comes back to them, as if one had touched a spring in a hidden cupboard of the memory, and out it all comes. I've seen that happen over and over again when I was doing my war work.

Reincarnation: If you can't believe in reincarnation – it is very helpful if you can – but, if not, just leave it alone. Some who have passed over become voluntarily reincarnated; it is an easier way of atoning for their faults than they could find over here. That's the reason, darling, why some people instinctively know why a thing is wrong for them to do. For instance, not to touch strong drink, because they suffered so dreadfully from the effects of strong drink in some other existence, they would not touch it now for anything...Don't worry about reincarnation, Mother. It doesn't matter a wee bit whether reincarnation is true or not true.

Time: Supposing I'd got no one I loved on the earth plane, and were only interested in the spirit world. I should have no sense of time at all, as we have no seasons here, and no night, and no day...We've got nothing, and I'm very glad, too, as we don't feel limited by time. and when I do anything I like doing it to the best of my ability. So you see, if I were only on my own sphere without visiting the earth plane, years might go on without any idea of how long it was...I come to you and I can sense whether it is light or dark on your plane – now I can. I couldn't at first, you know. And I can also tell time by you.

Spirit Presence: The earth plane always has many visitors from the spirit world, and when certain psychic people sense those spirits round about, they think, "Oh, they must always be here – the two worlds intermingle." Within a radius of a few miles from where you're sitting now, there'll be thousands and thousands of spirits, not all going to see someone, but engaged in uplifting work of some kind.

Passing Through Matter: Now, my body is composed of atoms, certainly of a different kind than the brick, just as your body is composed of different atoms than the brick; but my body is more purely etheric than yours, and the actual atoms are finer, simply because there is more ether in my body, so the atoms get through the spaces in the brick; that is the ether in the brick allows my atoms to penetrate it; so that if you saw me at the exact second I passed through the brick – it doesn't take a second, as a matter of fact, a hundredth part of a second, but if you could see it, you would see that the brick contains many more atoms of matter than before I entered it.

EPILOGUE

A MOTHER WITHOUT GRIEF

Extracted from "The Light Beyond" by Maurice Maeterlinck, a Belgian playwright, poet, and essayist who won the 1911 Nobel Prize in Literature

The other day I went to see a woman whom I knew before the war – she was happy then – and who had lost her only son in one of the battles in the Argonne. She was a widow, almost a poor woman; and, now that this son, her pride and joy, was no more, she no longer had any reason for living. I hesitated to knock on her door. Was I not about to witness one of those hopeless griefs at whose feet all words fall to the ground like shameful and insulting lies? Which of us today is not familiar with these mournful interviews, this dismal duty?

To my great astonishment, she handed me her hand with a kindly smile. Her eyes, to which I hardly dared raise my own, were free of tears.

"You have come to speak of him," she said, in a cheerful tone, and it was as if her voice had grown younger.

"Alas, yes! I had heard of your sorrow, and I have come...."

"Yes, I too believed that my unhappiness was irreparable; but now I know that he is not dead."

"What! He is not dead? Do you mean that the news...? But I thought that the body..."

"Yes, his body is over there; and I have even a photograph of the grave. Let me show it to you. See, that fourth cross on the left, that fourth cross; that is where he is lying. One of his friends, who buried him, sent me this card and gave me all the details. He suffered no pain. There was not even a death struggle. And he has told me so himself. He is quite astonished that death should be so easy, so slight a thing... You do not understand? Yes, I see what it is; you are just as I used to be, as all the others are. I do not explain the matter to the others; what would be the use? They do not wish to understand. But you, you will understand. He is more alive than he ever was; he is free and happy. He does just as he likes. He tells me that one cannot imagine what a release death is, what a weight it removes from you, nor the joy which it brings. He comes to see me when I call him. He loves, especially, to come in the evening; and we chat as we used to. He has not altered; he is just as he was on the day he went away, only younger, stronger, handsomer. We have never been happier, more united, nearer to one another. He divines my thoughts before I utter them. He knows everything; he sees everything; but he cannot tell me everything he knows. He maintains that I must be wanting to follow him and that I must wait for my hour. And, while I wait, we are living in a happiness greater than that which was ours before the war, a happiness which nothing can ever trouble again.

Those about her pitied the poor woman; and, as she did not weep, as she was gay and smiling, they believed her mad.

WAR AND PSYCHICAL PHENOMENA

"**M**an will assuredly outgrow war, with increasing knowledge and spiritual development," wrote Hereward Carrington, Ph.D., in his 1919 book, *Psychical Phenomena and The War*. If Carrington (1880-1958) is viewing things from his present realm of existence, he must be shaking his head in dismay and disgust at the lack of progress over the 95 years since he wrote those words.

An early chapter of the book is devoted to the psychology of the soldier. "It is a psychological fact of great importance and significance, that those at the front have the greatest confidence," he wrote. "The nearer the front we penetrate, the greater this feeling of confidence becomes." In his research during WWI, Carrington observed that there seems to be little fear of death on the front lines, that nearly every soldier feels a sort of inner conviction that he will not be killed – that fortune will shine upon him. The instinct of self-preservation takes over. "All the centuries of intervening civilization are swept away in an instant; and we see before us, not the cultured gentleman of yesterday, but the primitive brute-beast, fighting for his existence and his life precisely the same way that his ancestors fought – and with no other, higher ideals in mind! It shows us at once and graphically the effects upon the mind of war – and proves to us that it leads, not only to material destruction, and to mental and moral deterioration, but also to the very extinction of the spirit of man himself – in the almost instant reversion of civilized man to savagery."

Carrington went on to document prophecies and premonitions concerning the war, apparitions and dreams of soldiers, clairvoyant descriptions of death, and communication from soldiers who have "died." Here are a few of those stories, anecdotal, but interesting nonetheless:

A Premonition of Death: During the campaign on the Gallipoli Peninsula in 1915, Private Reynolds, a New Zealand foot soldier, awoke with a start from his sleep in the trench. He told his mate, Private Pugh, "I shall have to go on listening post duty at midnight on the 25th of June, and I shall be shot through the head." Pugh asked him to explain. "I had a dream just now, and in that dream I saw my mother reading a newspaper," Reynolds related. "She looked up from it suddenly, and her face was so white and her eyes so horror-struck that I found myself looking over her shoulder to see what she had been reading, and there in the 'roll of honor' my name stood out – 'Private Reynolds, shot through the head while on listening post duty on June 25,' is what I read."

Pugh laughed and joked about it with other chums in the unit. They said his dream was the result of fatigue and bad food. However, several days later, on June 25, Private Reynolds was assigned listening post duty and was shot through the head. The officer in charge of the unit confirmed the story.

The Ghost of Private Rex: A Lieutenant Smith was marching his unit from one place to another. Suddenly he saw Private Rex falling behind. Smith confronted Rex and asked him if he were hungry. The private responded, "A little." The officer gave him a malted milk tablet and took note of the fact that Rex's hand was icy cold and that he was very pale. The officer's attention was diverted and when he returned to check on Rex he was gone. Another officer reminded Smith that Rex had been killed in battle three days earlier. Smith told Carrington that because of the stresses of subsequent fighting and of the death of so many others, he had momentarily forgotten. However, he was emphatic that he had seen, talked to, and touched Private Rex that evening. "It takes away all the fear of death," Smith said, "for I know that Private Rex lives, though dead."

The Pearl Tie-Pin Case: Geraldine Cummins had a cousin, a British army officer, who had been killed in battle in France a month before she sat at the Ouija board and saw her cousin's name unexpectedly spelled out. After some identifying exchanges, the following message came: "Tell mother to give my pearl tie-pin to the girl I was going to marry, I think she ought to have it." Miss Cummins asked her cousin to give her the name and address of the young lady. The full Christian and surname were spelled out, the latter being a very unusual one and unknown to both sitters. The address turned out to be wrong or incorrectly recorded by the sitters as a letter sent there was returned, and the whole message was thought to be fictitious.

Six months later, it was determined that the officer had been engaged to the very lady whose name was given. However, he had told no one. It wasn't until the War Office had sent over the deceased officer's effects that relatives found the woman's name in his will and as his next of kin. It was exactly as given on the Ouija board. Equally remarkable was the fact that a pearl tie-pin was also found in his effects.

Editor's note: Geraldine Cummins, a famous automatic writing medium, is discussed in the Introduction of this anthology. She was referred to in Carrington's book only as "Miss C." as she was just 17 at the time and not yet developed as a medium.

Apparition in the Trenches: A very popular commanding officer of a British regiment was badly wounded in battle, losing an arm. Upon returning home, he was fitted with an artificial arm and felt he was well enough to rejoin his regiment. His request to do so was denied, but he was offered a post in the Dardanelles. Shortly after arriving there, he contracted a severe case of dysentery, and was sent home in a hospital train. At the very moment of his death in the hospital train, he appeared to his old regiment in the trenches of Flanders. The sergeant-major of one of the regiment's companies was surprised to see the colonel and commented to a company commander that the colonel was back. As the company commander was about to greet the colonel, the colonel disappeared. The apparition of the colonel is said to have been witnessed by many other soldiers present that day.

Sapper Kelly finds 32 wells: The absence of water was the biggest obstacle facing the allied forces in holding their position on the Gallipoli peninsula. Military engineers had sunk shafts in search of water but without success. The heat was intense and a complete breakdown was threatened when the generals in command heard of Sapper Kelly's reputation as a dowser. Kelly was a member of the Australian Expeditionary Forces. Carrying a small piece of copper in his hands, Kelly located 32 wells, on which pumps were subsequently erected. He was able to say whether it was merely a pocket of water, a spring, or an underground river.

Victims of the Lusitania

Certainly, not all of the casualties in the Great War were soldiers. Here are two interesting stories about civilians aboard the *RMS Lusitania*, a passenger ship sunk May 7, 1915 by a torpedo from a German U-boat about 14 miles off the coast of southern Ireland as it sailed from New York City to Liverpool.

On May 7, 1915, Hester Travers Smith was sitting at the Ouija board with Lennox Robinson, a world-renowned Irish playwright. Both were blindfolded as the Rev. Savell Hicks sat between them and copied the letters indicated by the board's "traveler."

"Pray for Hugh Lane," was the first message received. Following the prayer request, the traveler spelled out: "I am Hugh Lane, all is dark." At that point, however, Travers Smith and Robinson were still blindfolded and had no idea as to the message. In fact, they were conversing on other matters as their hands moved rapidly. After several minutes, Hicks told Travers Smith and Robinson that it was Sir Hugh Lane coming through and that he told them he was aboard the *Lusitania* and had drowned.

On her way home that evening, Travers Smith had heard about the sinking of the passenger ship by a German torpedo, but she had not yet read the details, nor did she or the others know that Sir Hugh Lane was a passenger on the ship sailing from New York to England. In her 1919 book, *Voices from the Void*, Travers Smith states that she knew Lane and had heard that he had gone to New York, but it never occurred to her when she heard of the sinking that he was on board.

While distressed, they continued receiving messages from Lane, who told them that there was panic, the life boats were lowered, and the women went first. He went on to say that he was the last to get in an overcrowded life boat, fell over, and lost all memory until he "saw a light" at their sitting. To establish his identity, Lane gave Travers Smith an evidential message about the last time they had met and talked, although when Travers Smith asked for his cabin number on the ship as proof that it was Lane communicating, the number given to her was later discovered to be incorrect. She reasoned, however, that he was in a confused state and that it is not unusual for people to forget their cabin numbers. Nor is it unusual for boat passengers to remember where their cabin is located without memorizing the number.

"I did not suffer. I was drowned and felt nothing," Lane further communicated that night. He also gave intimate messages for friends of his in Dublin.

Lane, 39 at the time of his death, was an art connoisseur and director of the National Gallery of Ireland in Dublin. He was transporting lead containers with paintings of Monet, Rembrandt, Rubens, and Titian, which were insured for $4 million and were to be displayed at the National Gallery. It was reported by survivors that Lane was seen on deck looking out to Ireland before going down to the dining saloon just before the torpedoes struck.

Lane continued to communicate at subsequent sittings. As plans were underway to erect a memorial gallery to him, he begged that Travers Smith let those behind the movement know that he did not want such a memorial. However, he was more concerned that a codicil to his will be honored. He had left his private collection of art to the National Gallery in London, but the codicil stated that they should go to the National Gallery in Dublin. Because he had not signed the codicil, the London gallery was reluctant to give them up. "Those pictures must be secured for Dublin," Lane communicated on January 22, 1918, going on to say that he could not rest until they were.

At a sitting that September, Sir William Barrett, a distinguished British physicist and psychical researcher, was present. Prior to the sitting, Travers Smith and Barrett discussed how evidential the messages from Lane were to them, although they could understand why the public doubted. After the sitting started, a man who said he had died in Sheffield communicated first. Then, Travers Smith recalled, Robinson's arm was seized and driven about so forcibly that the traveler fell off the table more than once. It was Lane, who was upset because of the doubts expressed relative to his communication. W. B. Yeats, the famous poet, also reported contact with Lane, his close friend, through a medium in London. He said that the medium told him that a drowned man followed him into the room and then went on to describe a scene at the bottom of the sea.

In the Appendix of his 1916 classic, *Raymond or Life and Death* (See Chapter One), Sir Oliver Lodge tells of a friend bringing one of the *RMS Lusitania* survivors for a visit to his Mariemont home near Edgbaston in England.

Lodge was fascinated with the woman's account of the ordeal. "I found her a charming person, and she entered into the matter with surprising fullness, considering that she was a complete stranger," the distinguished British physicist and educator wrote.

The woman recalled being sucked down by the ship, then coming to the surface with the feeling of blank surprise at the disappearance of the huge vessel. Lodge found her account so interesting that he later wrote to her and asked her if she would write down in as much detail as possible her recollection of the event so that he could include it in the book. The woman complied, but asked that her name not be disclosed.

"I have always remembered the sympathy with which you listened to me that morning at Egdbaston, and sometimes wondered at the amount I said," the survivor responded to Lodge, "as it is not easy to give expression to feelings and speculations which are only roused in critical moments in one's life.

"What you ask me to do is not easy, as I am only one of those who are puzzling and groping in the dark – while you have found so much light for yourself and have imparted it to others."

The woman recalled having a premonition of the tragedy. "It was not a very actual knowledge, but I was conscious of a distinct forewarning, and the very calmness and peace of the voyage seemed, in a way, a state of waiting for some great event. Therefore, when the ship was rent by the explosion, I felt no particular shock, because of that curious inner expectancy."

She put down her book and went to the other side of the ship where many passengers were gathering around the life boats with no panic whatsoever. The ship was listing heavily and it was already difficult to stand. She returned to her cabin, where a steward helped her put on a life-jacket and advised her to discard her fur coat. "I felt no hurry or anxiety, and returned on deck, where I stood with some difficulty."

The woman remembered talking to an elderly man about their chances of survival. "It was then I think we realized what a strong instinct there was in some of us – not to struggle madly for life – but to wait for something to come to us, whether it be life or death; and not to lose our personality and become like one of the struggling shouting creatures who were by then swarming up from the lower decks and made one's heart ache." She wondered if the "grim calmness" was part of some "desire to die" instinct.

"I never felt for a moment that my time to cross over had come – not until I found myself in the water – floating farther and farther away from the scene of wreckage and misery – in a sea as calm and vast as the sky overhead."

Behind her, she heard the cries of others, the splashing of oars, and the calls of those doing rescue work from the lifeboats. "There seemed to be no possibility of rescue for me, so I reasoned with myself and said, 'The time has come – you must believe it – the time to cross over' – but inwardly and persistently something continued to say, 'No, not now.'"

Continuing to drift away from the pandemonium, the woman observed gulls flying overhead and took note of the blue shadows the sea threw up from their white feathers. She began to feel lonely as her thoughts turned to her loved ones who were awaiting her arrival. "The idea of their grief was unbearable, and I had to cry a little." She recalled the names of books rushing through her brain, especially one titled "Where no Fear is" as representing her feelings at the time. "Loneliness, yes, and sorrow on account of the grief of others – but no fear. It seemed very normal – very right – a natural development of some kind about to take place. How can it be otherwise, when it is natural? I rather wished I knew some one on the other side, and wondered if there are friendly strangers there who come to the rescue.

"The woman recalled feeling "near the borderline" when a lifeboat came up behind her and two men bent down to lift her in. "It was extraordinary how quickly life came rushing back; everyone in the boat seemed very self-possessed, although there was one man dead and another losing his reason. One woman expressed a hope for a cup to tea."

A minesweeper from Queenstown soon picked them up. "I am glad to have been near the border," the woman concluded her remarks to Sir Oliver, "to have had the feeling of how very near it is always – only there are so many little things always going on to absorb one here.

"Others on that day were passing through a Gate which was not open for me – but I do not expect they were afraid when the time came – they too probably felt that whatever they were to find would be beautiful – only a fulfillment of some kind…I have reason to think that the passing from here is very painless – at least where there is no illness. We seemed to be passing through a stage on the road to Life."

REFERENCES

Barker, Elsa, *War Letters From The Living Dead Man*, White Crow Books, UK, 2009

Barrett, Sir William, *On the Threshold of the Unseen*, E.F. Dutton & Co., New York, 1917

Barrett, Lady Florence, *Personality Survives Death*, Longmans, Green and Co., London, 1937

Berger, Arthur S. and Joyce, *The Encyclopedia of Parapsychology and Psychical Research*, Paragon House, 1991

Boylan, Grace Duffie, *Thy Son Liveth: Messages from a Soldier to his Mother*, Little, Brown, & Co., Boston, 1918

Budreau, Lisa M. *Bodies of War*, New York University Press, New York & London

Carrington, Hereward, *Psychical Phenomena and the War*, Dodd, Mead and Co., New York, 1919

Cummins, Geraldine, *The Road to Immortality*, The Aquarian Publishing Co., London, 1932

Cummins, Geraldine, *Unseen Adventures*, Rider and Company, London, 1951

Cummins, Geraldine, *Mind in Life and Death*, The Aquarian Press, London, 1956

Cummins, Geraldine, *They Survive*, Psychic Book Club, London, no date

Davis, Andrew Jackson, *Death and the After Life*, Colby and Rich, Boston, 1865

Doyle, Arthur Conan, *The Vital Message*, George H. Doran Company, New York, 1919

Doyle, Arthur Conan, M.D., LL.D., *The History of Spiritualism*, George H. Doran Company, New York, 1926

Doyle, Arthur Conan, *Pheneas Speaks*, George H. Doran Co., New York, 1927

Duffey, Mrs. E. B., *Heaven Revised*, Two Worlds Publishing Co., Manchester, UK, 1921

Eddy, Sherwood, *You Will Survive Death*, The Omega Press, Surrey, England, 1954

Edmonds, John W., and Dexter, George T., *Spiritualism*, Partridge & Brittan, New York, 1853

Greber, Johannes, *Communication with The Spirit World of God*, Johannes Greber Memorial Foundation, Teaneck, NJ, 1979

Hamilton, Trevor, *Immortal Longings*, Imprint-Academic.com, Exeter, UK, 2009

Harding, Emma, *Modern American Spiritualism*, University Books, New Hyde Park, NY, 1970 (reprint of 1869 book)

Hare, Robert, M.D., *Experimental Investigation of the Spirit Manifestations*, Partridge & Brittan, New York, 1855

Holt, Henry, *On the Cosmic Relations*, Houghton Mifflin Company, Boston and New York, 1914

Hyslop, James H., *Contact with the Other World*, The Century Co., New York, 1919

Kardec, Allan, *The Spirits' Book*, Amapse Society, Mexico, reprint from 1857

Kardec, Allan, *The Book on Mediums*, Samuel Weiser, Inc., York Beach, Maine (reprint of 1874 book)

Kelway-Bamber, L., *Claude's Book*, Psychic Book Club, London, originally published in 1919

Kelway-Banber, *L. Claude's Second Book*, http://spiritwritings.com/claude2.pdf

Leonard, Gladys Osborne, *My Life in Two Worlds*, Cassell & Company, Ltd., London, 1931

Leonard, Gladys Osborne, *The Last Crossing*, Psychic Book Club, London, 1937

Little, Nelly, *Rolf's Life in the Spirit World*, (publisher and publication date not listed)

Lodge, Oliver, *The Survival of Man*, Moffat, Yard and Co., New York, 1909

Lodge, Sir Oliver, *Raymond or Life and Death*, George H. Doran Company, New York, NY, 1916

Lodge, Sir Oliver, *Raymond Revised*, Methuen & Co. Ltd., 1922

Lodge, Oliver, Past Years, *Charles Scribner's Sons*, New York, 1932

Maeterlinck, Maurice, *The Light Beyond*, Dodd, Mead, and Co., New York, 1918

Moses, William Stainton, *Spirit Teachings*, Arno Press, New York,1976, reprinted from 1924 edition published by London Spiritualist Alliance

Moses, William Stainton, *More Spirit Teachings*, Meilach.com

Myers, F. W. H., *Human Personality and its Survival of Bodily Death*, University Books, Inc., New Hyde Park, NY, 1961 (reprint of 1903 book)

Naylor, William, *Silver Birch Anthology*, Spiritualist Press, London, 1955

Ortzen, Tony, *The Seed of Truth*, The Spiritual Truth Press, Surrey, UK, 1987

Owen, G. Vale, *The Life Beyond The Veil*, George H. Doran Co., New York, 1921

Prince, Walter Franklin, *The Case of Patience Worth*, University Books, New Hyde Park, NY., 1964 (original from Boston Society for Psychic Research, 1927)

Rosher. Grace. *Beyond the Horizon*, James Clarke & Co., London, 1961

Rosher, Grace, *The Travellers' Return*, Psychic Press, Ltd., London, 1968

Scott, John, *As One Ghost to Another*, Spiritualist Press Ltd., London, 1948

Smith, Susy, *The Book of James*, G. P. Putnam's Sons, New York, 1974

Smith, Suzy, *the Afterlife Codes*, Hampton Roads, Charlottesville, VA, 2000

Stead, William T., *After Death or Letters from Julia*, The Progressive Thinker Publishing House, 1909 (reprinted by Kessinger Publishing, LLC)

Thomas, Charles Drayton, *Life Beyond Death with Evidence*, W. Collins Sons. & Co., Glasgow, 1928

Thomas, Charles Drayton, *Some New Evidence for Human Survival*, Spiritualist Press Ltd., London, 1922

Travers Smith, Hester, *Voices from the Void*, E. P. Dutton & Company, New York, 1919

Tudor Pole, Wellesley, *Private Dowding*, Pilgrims Book Service, Norwich, England, 1917

Tweedale, Charles L., *Man's Survival After Death*, Psychic book Club, London, 1925

Wallace, Alfred Russel, *Miracles and Modern Spiritualism*, George Redway, London, 1896

Wetzel, Joseph, *The Bridge Over the River*, Anthroposophic Press, 1974

Whiting, Lilian, *The Spiritual Significance*, Little, Brown, & Co., Boston, 1901

Wood, Frederic H , *Through the Psychic Door*, Psychic Book Club, London, 1954

Wood, Frederic H., *Mediumship and War*, Rider & Co., London, year not stated

Paperbacks also available from
White Crow Books

Elsa Barker—*Letters from
a Living Dead Man*
ISBN 978-1-907355-83-7

Elsa Barker—*War Letters from
the Living Dead Man*
ISBN 978-1-907355-85-1

Elsa Barker—*Last Letters from
the Living Dead Man*
ISBN 978-1-907355-87-5

Richard Maurice Bucke—
Cosmic Consciousness
ISBN 978-1-907355-10-3

Arthur Conan Doyle—
The Edge of the Unknown
ISBN 978-1-907355-14-1

Arthur Conan Doyle—
The New Revelation
ISBN 978-1-907355-12-7

Arthur Conan Doyle—
The Vital Message
ISBN 978-1-907355-13-4

Arthur Conan Doyle with
Simon Parke—*Conversations
with Arthur Conan Doyle*
ISBN 978-1-907355-80-6

Meister Eckhart with Simon Parke—
Conversations with Meister Eckhart
ISBN 978-1-907355-18-9

D. D. Home—*Incidents in my Life Part 1*
ISBN 978-1-907355-15-8

Mme. Dunglas Home; edited,
with an Introduction, by Sir
Arthur Conan Doyle—*D. D.
Home: His Life and Mission*
ISBN 978-1-907355-16-5

Edward C. Randall—
Frontiers of the Afterlife
ISBN 978-1-907355-30-1

Rebecca Ruter Springer—
Intra Muros: My Dream of Heaven
ISBN 978-1-907355-11-0

Leo Tolstoy, edited by Simon
Parke—*Forbidden Words*
ISBN 978-1-907355-00-4

Leo Tolstoy—*A Confession*
ISBN 978-1-907355-24-0

Leo Tolstoy—*The Gospel in Brief*
ISBN 978-1-907355-22-6

Leo Tolstoy—*The Kingdom
of God is Within You*
ISBN 978-1-907355-27-1

Leo Tolstoy—*My Religion:
What I Believe*
ISBN 978-1-907355-23-3

Leo Tolstoy—*On Life*
ISBN 978-1-907355-91-2

Leo Tolstoy—*Twenty-three Tales*
ISBN 978-1-907355-29-5

Leo Tolstoy—*What is Religion
and other writings*
ISBN 978-1-907355-28-8

Leo Tolstoy—*Work While
Ye Have the Light*
ISBN 978-1-907355-26-4

Leo Tolstoy—*The Death of Ivan Ilyich*
ISBN 978-1-907661-10-5

Leo Tolstoy—*Resurrection*
ISBN 978-1-907661-09-9

Leo Tolstoy with Simon Parke—
Conversations with Tolstoy
ISBN 978-1-907355-25-7

Howard Williams with an Introduction
by Leo Tolstoy—*The Ethics of Diet:
An Anthology of Vegetarian Thought*
ISBN 978-1-907355-21-9

Vincent Van Gogh with Simon
Parke—*Conversations with Van Gogh*
ISBN 978-1-907355-95-0

Wolfgang Amadeus Mozart with Simon
Parke—*Conversations with Mozart*
ISBN 978-1-907661-38-9

Jesus of Nazareth with Simon Parke—
Conversations with Jesus of Nazareth
ISBN 978-1-907661-41-9

Thomas à Kempis with Simon
Parke—*The Imitation of Christ*
ISBN 978-1-907661-58-7

Julian of Norwich with Simon
Parke—*Revelations of Divine Love*
ISBN 978-1-907661-88-4

Allan Kardec—*The Spirits Book*
ISBN 978-1-907355-98-1

Allan Kardec—*The Book on Mediums*
ISBN 978-1-907661-75-4

Emanuel Swedenborg—*Heaven and Hell*
ISBN 978-1-907661-55-6

P.D. Ouspensky—*Tertium Organum:
The Third Canon of Thought*
ISBN 978-1-907661-47-1

Dwight Goddard—*A Buddhist Bible*
ISBN 978-1-907661-44-0

Michael Tymn—*The Afterlife Revealed*
ISBN 978-1-970661-90-7

Michael Tymn—*Transcending the
Titanic: Beyond Death's Door*
ISBN 978-1-908733-02-3

Guy L. Playfair—*If This Be Magic*
ISBN 978-1-907661-84-6

Guy L. Playfair—*The Flying Cow*
ISBN 978-1-907661-94-5

Guy L. Playfair —*This House is Haunted*
ISBN 978-1-907661-78-5

Carl Wickland, M.D.—
Thirty Years Among the Dead
ISBN 978-1-907661-72-3

John E. Mack—*Passport to the Cosmos*
ISBN 978-1-907661-81-5

Peter & Elizabeth Fenwick—
The Truth in the Light
ISBN 978-1-908733-08-5

Erlendur Haraldsson—
Modern Miracles
ISBN 978-1-908733-25-2

Erlendur Haraldsson—
At the Hour of Death
ISBN 978-1-908733-27-6

Erlendur Haraldsson—
The Departed Among the Living
ISBN 978-1-908733-29-0

Brian Inglis—*Science and Parascience*
ISBN 978-1-908733-18-4

Brian Inglis—*Natural and Supernatural:
A History of the Paranormal*
ISBN 978-1-908733-20-7

Ernest Holmes—*The Science of Mind*
ISBN 978-1-908733-10-8

Victor & Wendy Zammit —*A Lawyer
Presents the Evidence For the Afterlife*
ISBN 978-1-908733-22-1

Casper S. Yost—*Patience
Worth: A Psychic Mystery*
ISBN 978-1-908733-06-1

William Usborne Moore—
Glimpses of the Next State
ISBN 978-1-907661-01-3

William Usborne Moore—
The Voices
ISBN 978-1-908733-04-7

John W. White—
The Highest State of Consciousness
ISBN 978-1-908733-31-3

Stafford Betty—
The Imprisoned Splendor
ISBN 978-1-907661-98-3

Paul Pearsall, Ph.D. —
Super Joy
ISBN 978-1-908733-16-0

**All titles available as eBooks, and selected titles available in Hardback and
Audiobook formats from www.whitecrowbooks.com**